THE FAT CAT SHAT!

FOR ANYONE WITH A CAT AND A LITTERBOX

THE FAT CAT SHAT!

FOR ANYONE WITH A CAT AND A LITTERBOX

Julia M. Busch

ANTI-AGING PRESS, INC.

P.O. BOX 141489 • CORAL GABLES, FLORIDA • 33114

© Copyright 1995 book and illustrations by Julia M. Busch
All rights reserved.
First printing
Printed in the United States of America

Anti-Aging Press books are available at special discounts for bulk purchases for premiums, fund-raising, sales promotions or educational use. Special editions or book excerpts can be composed to specification. For details, contact:

Marketing Department
Anti-Aging Press
P.O. Box 141489
Coral Gables, FL 33114

Publisher's Cataloging in Publication

Busch, Julia M., 1940-
  The fat cat shat! : for anyone with a cat and a litterbox / Julia M. Busch.
   p. cm.
   Preassigned: LCCN: 94-78113
   ISBN 0-9632907-7-0

  1. Cats--Humor. 2. Scatology--Humor.   I. Title.

PN6231.C23B87 1995   818'.54
                                  QB194-2027

ANTI-AGING PRESS, INC.

P.O. BOX 141489 • CORAL GABLES, FLORIDA • 33114

To
All Cat Lovers
(*Have I got a "Scoop" for You!*)

THE "SCOOP!"

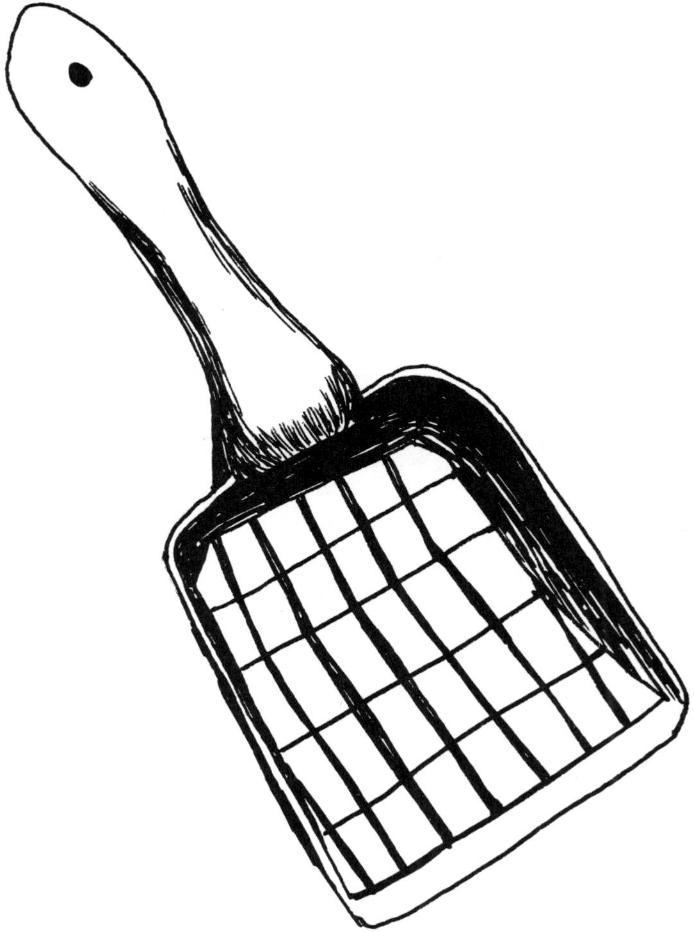

ACKNOWLEDGMENTS

Thank you Mary Jane for suggesting that I write a book on cats. It's the most fun I've had so far!

CONTENTS

One: THE FAT CAT SHAT!.....11

Two: CHRISTINE.....23

Three: LITTER-ICKS (LITTERBOX LIMERICKS) AND **OTHER TALES FROM THE "CRAPT"!**.....35

Four: LITTER-ally SPEAKING.....67

Five: SCATT-ILLOGICAL REFERENCES.....89

One:
THE FAT CAT SHAT!

**The Fat Cat Shat
in a
Famous Doctor's Hat!**

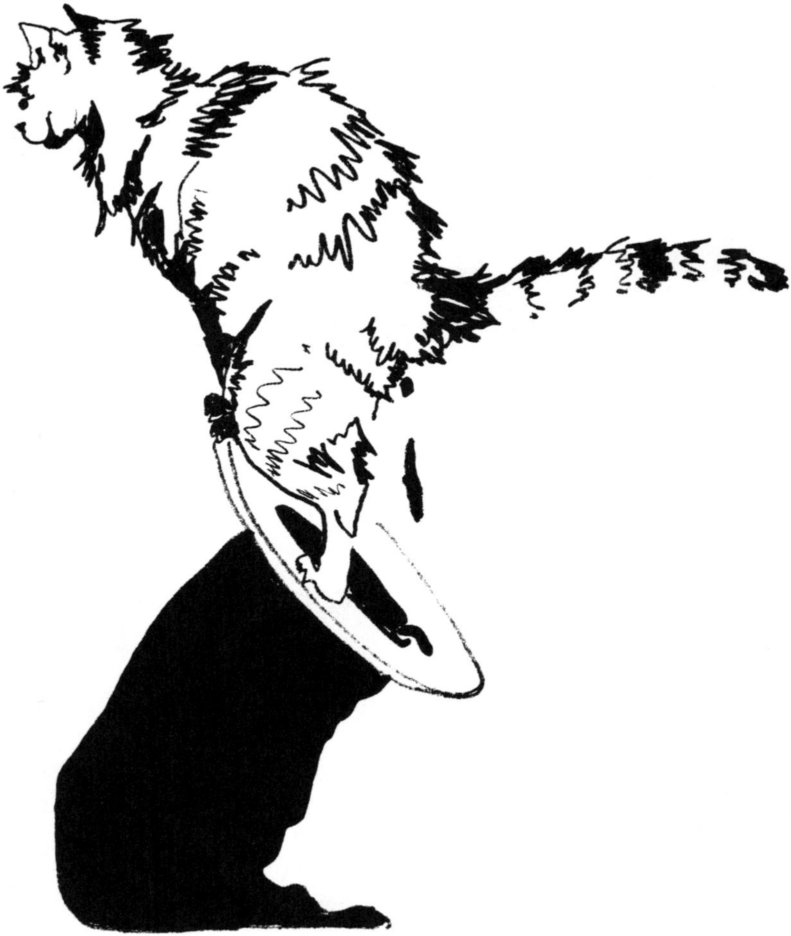

**He did it on
The front door mat.**

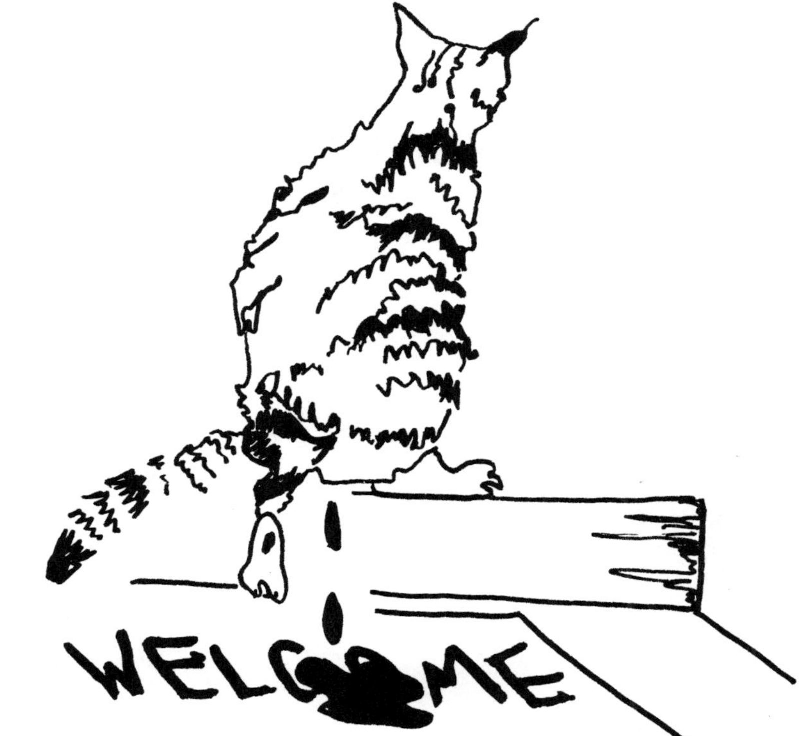
WELC ME

**And everywhere he squat,
It all went splat!**

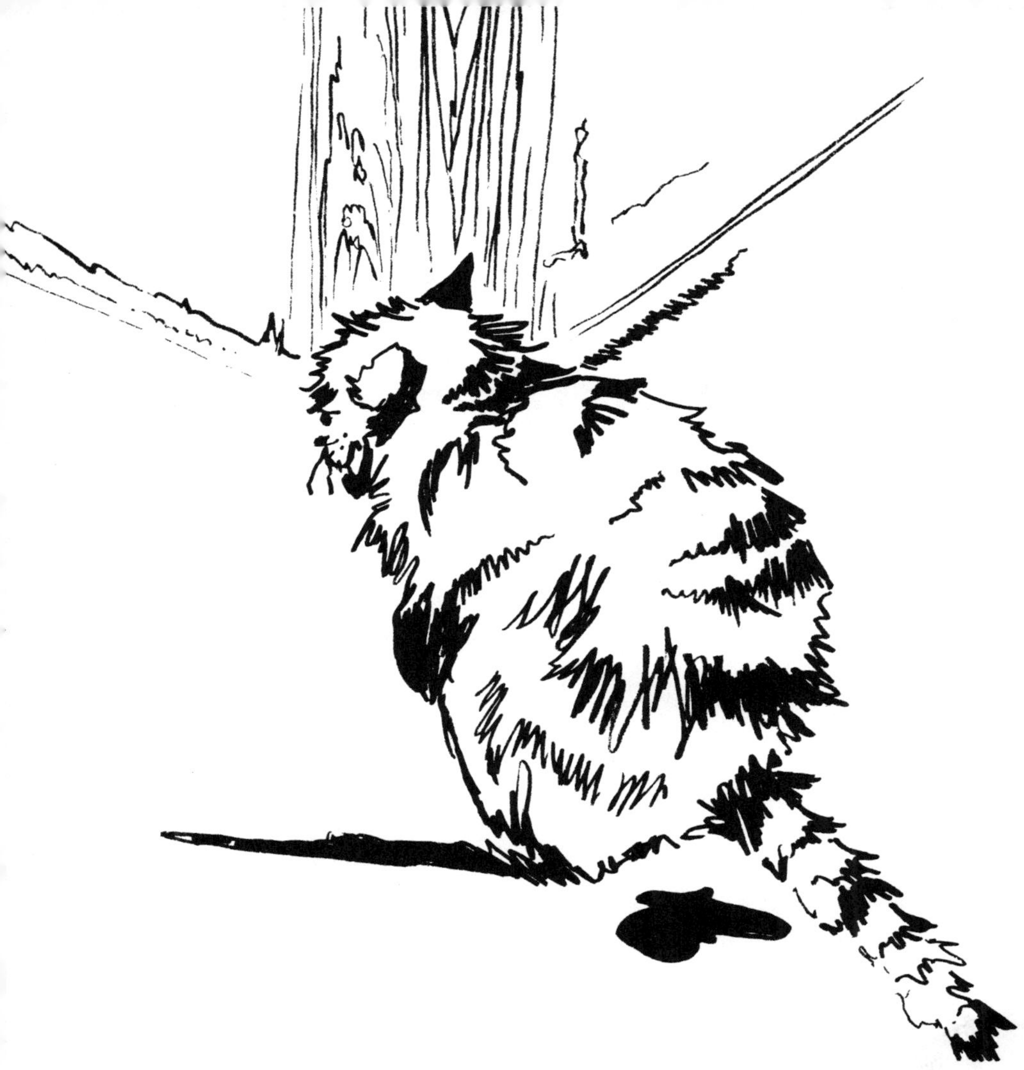

Got hold of a bad rat.

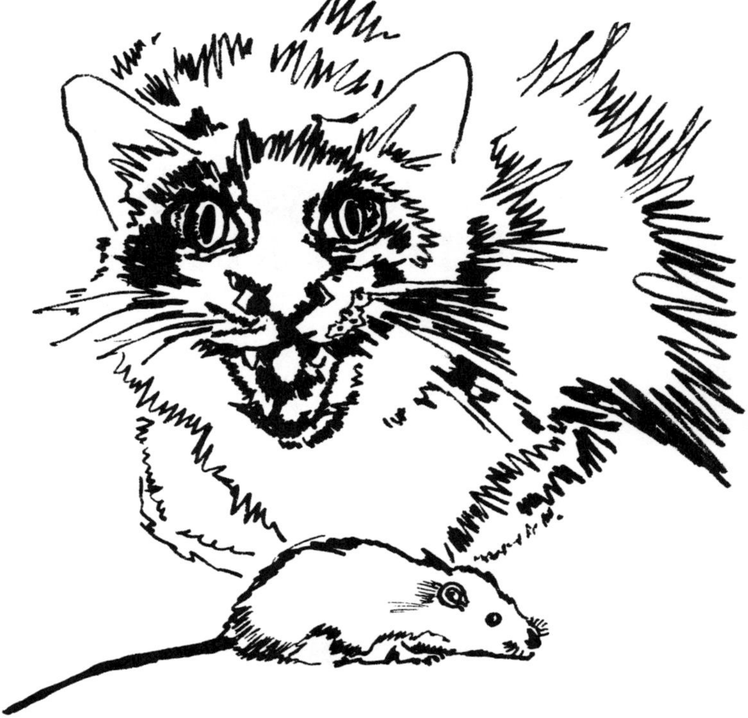

**A few more days of that,
His big belly will be flat!**

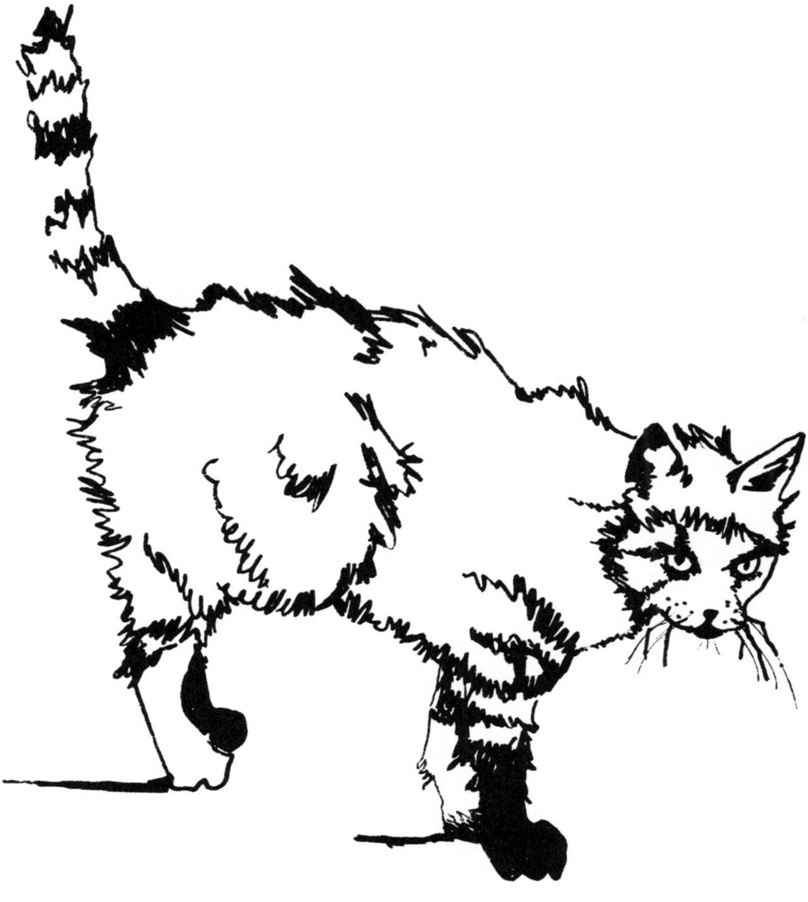

Two:
Christine

**Christine
Is an itinerant lass.**

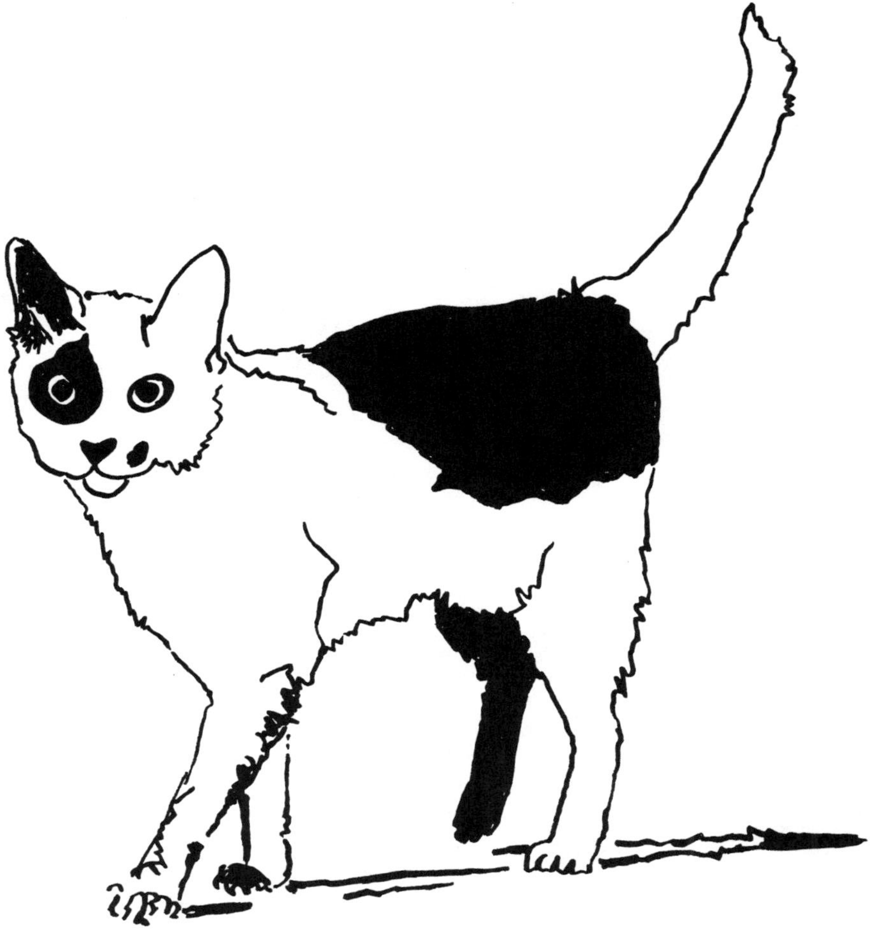

**Who loves to do it
In tall grass.**

**I think it's 'cause
It tickles her a_ _!**

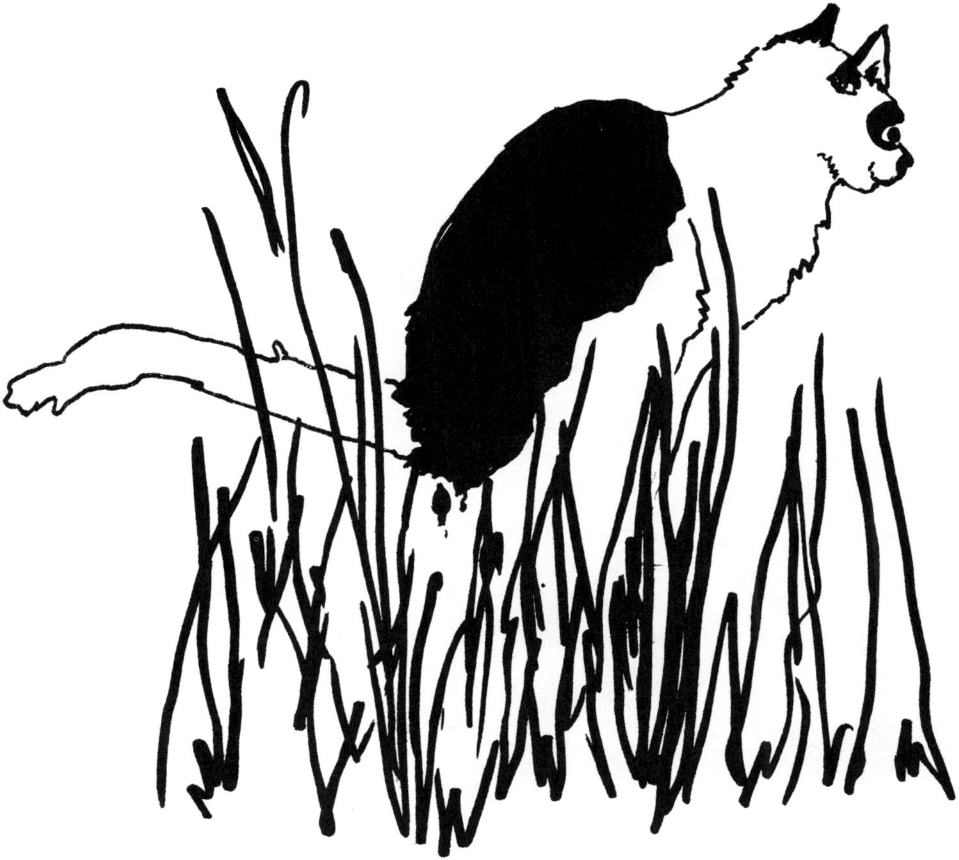

**But sometimes...
She'll just give a yawn.**

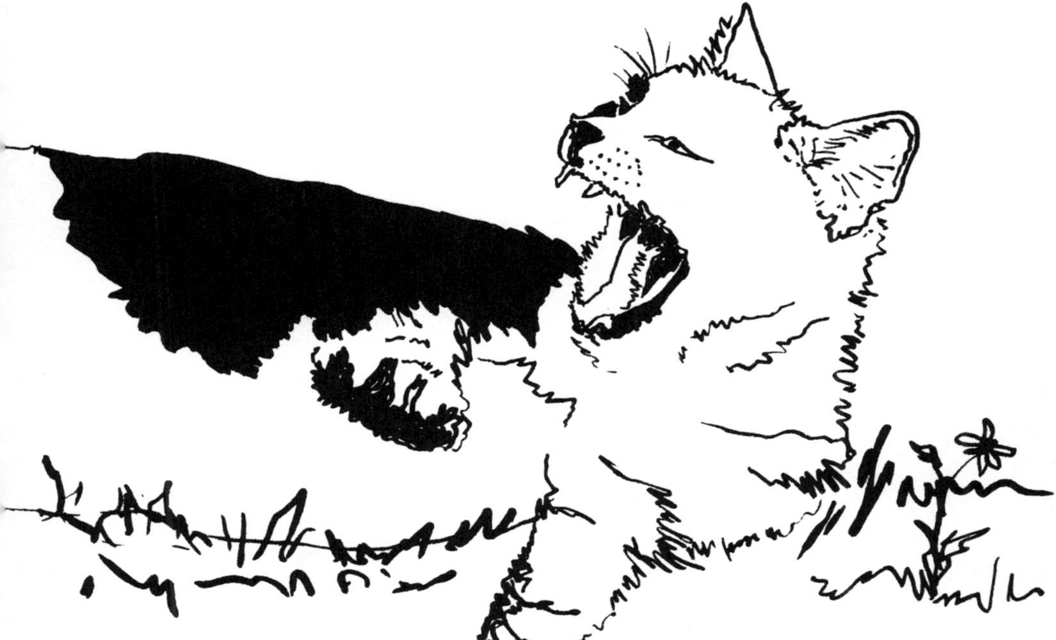

**And let one drop
In mid-front lawn!**

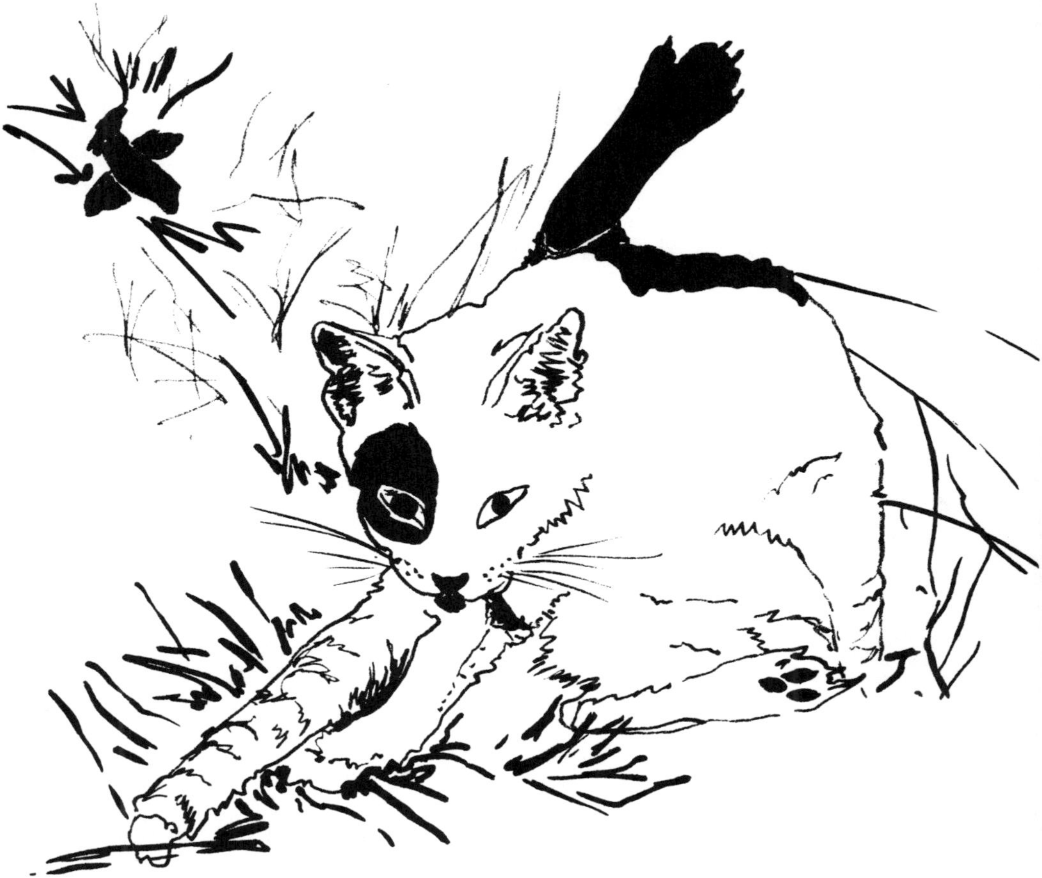

**Too tired for stimulation
I guess.**

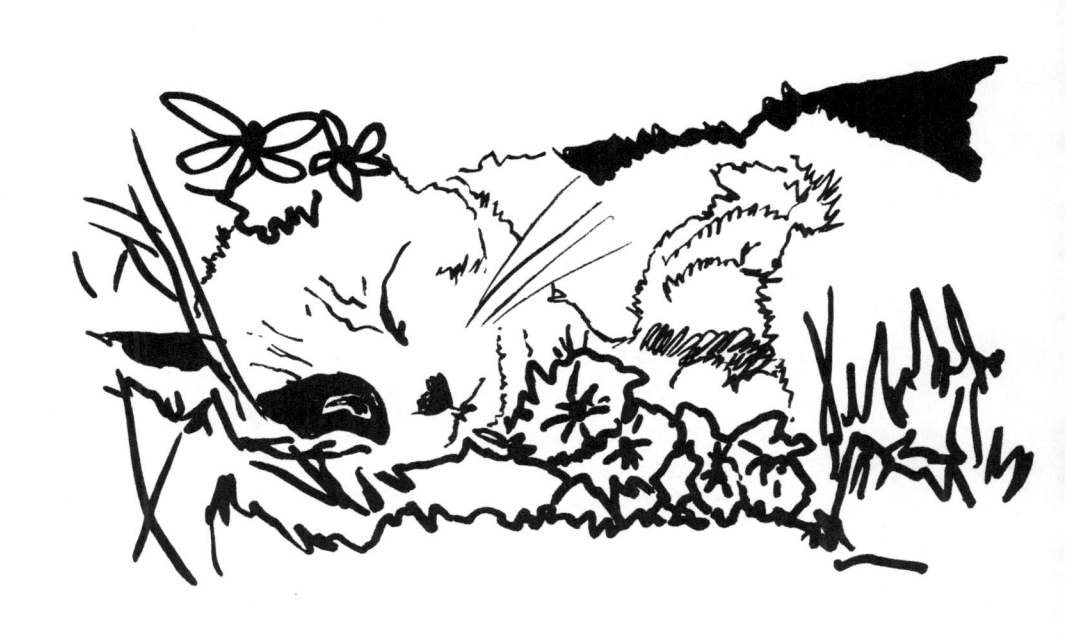

Three: LITTER-ICKS (LITTERBOX LIMERICKS) AND OTHER TALES FROM THE "CRAPT"!

"Yum-Yum"

**Yum-Yum is the
Perfect Tortie.**

**She boasts a coat
That's mighty sportie.**

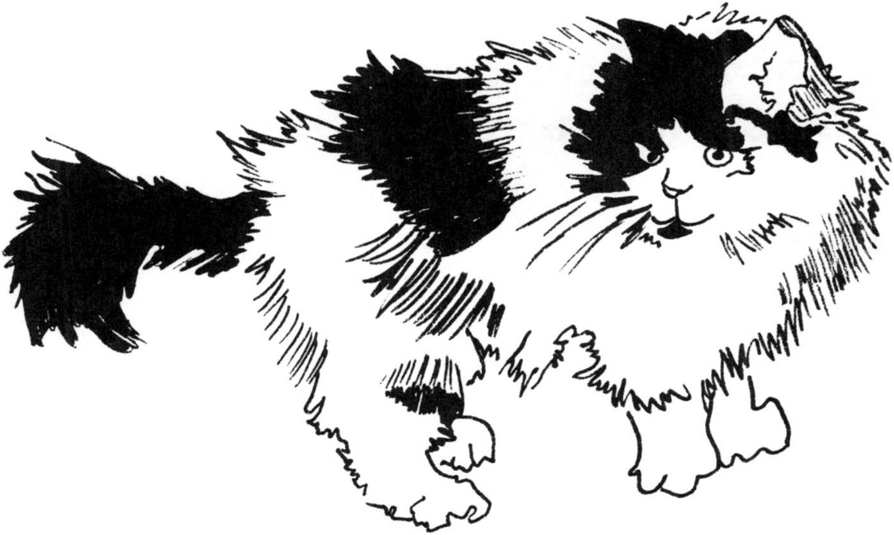

**But her technique in the litterbox
Comes up much too shortie!**

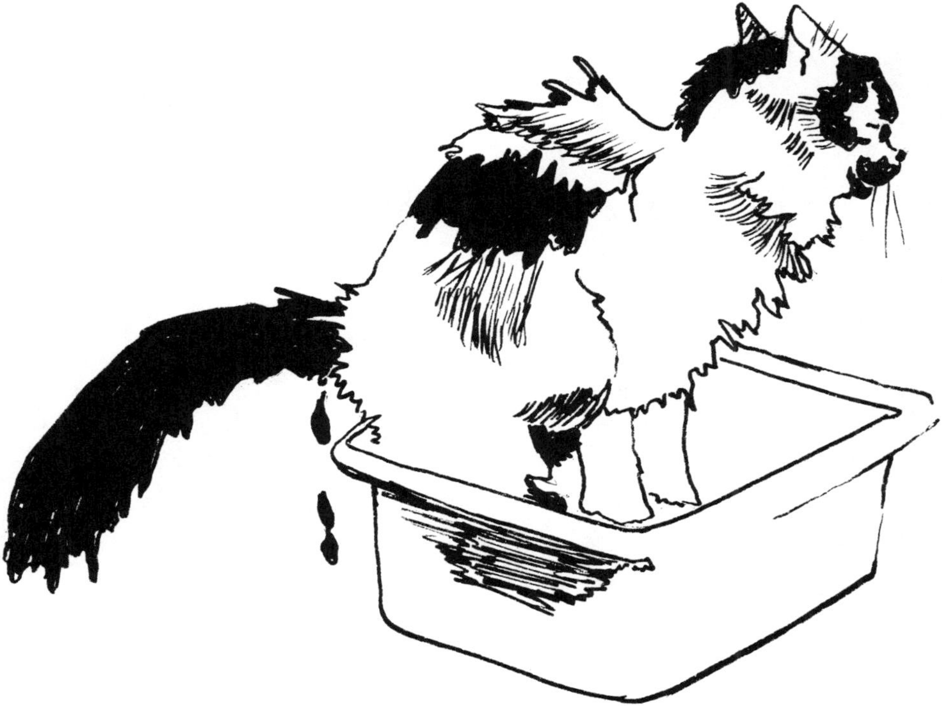

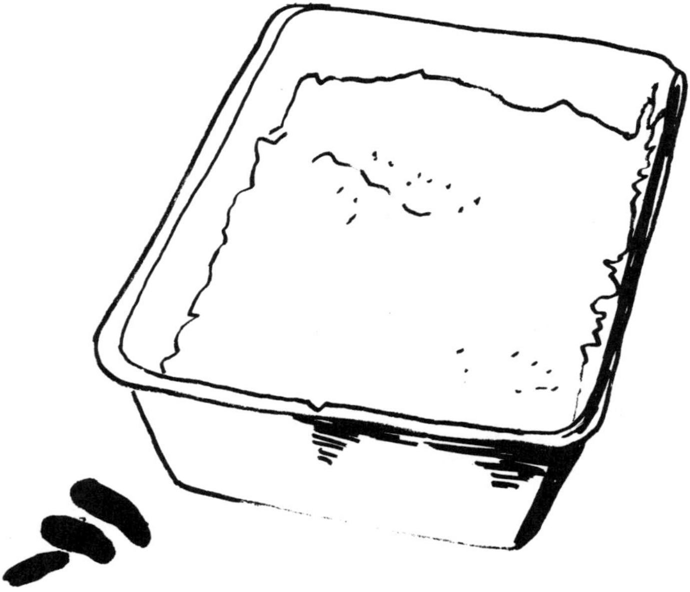

"Blackie"

A cat who we call "Blackie"
We think is a bit wackie.

He perches on the rim of the box
Just to do his kackie.

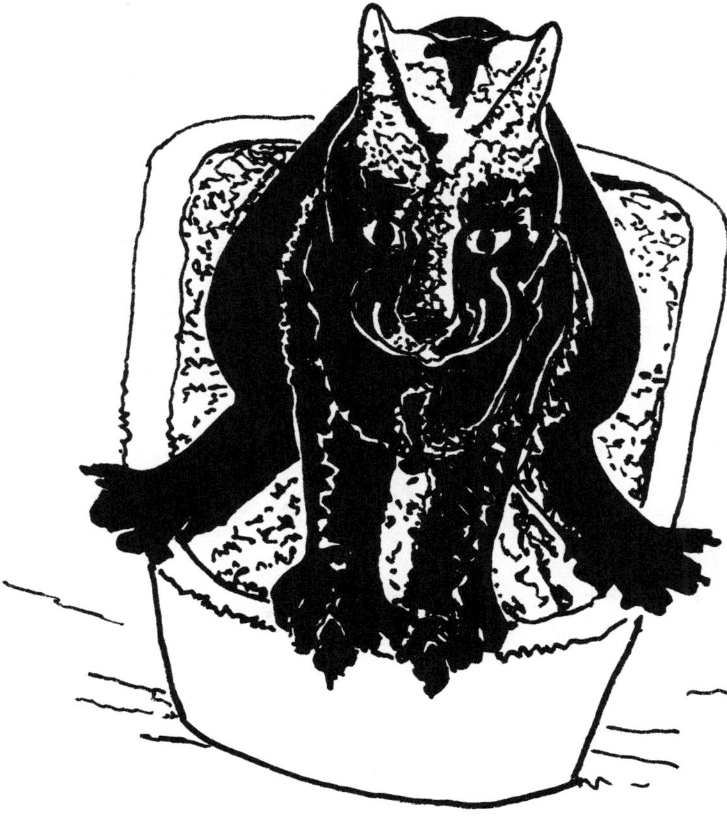

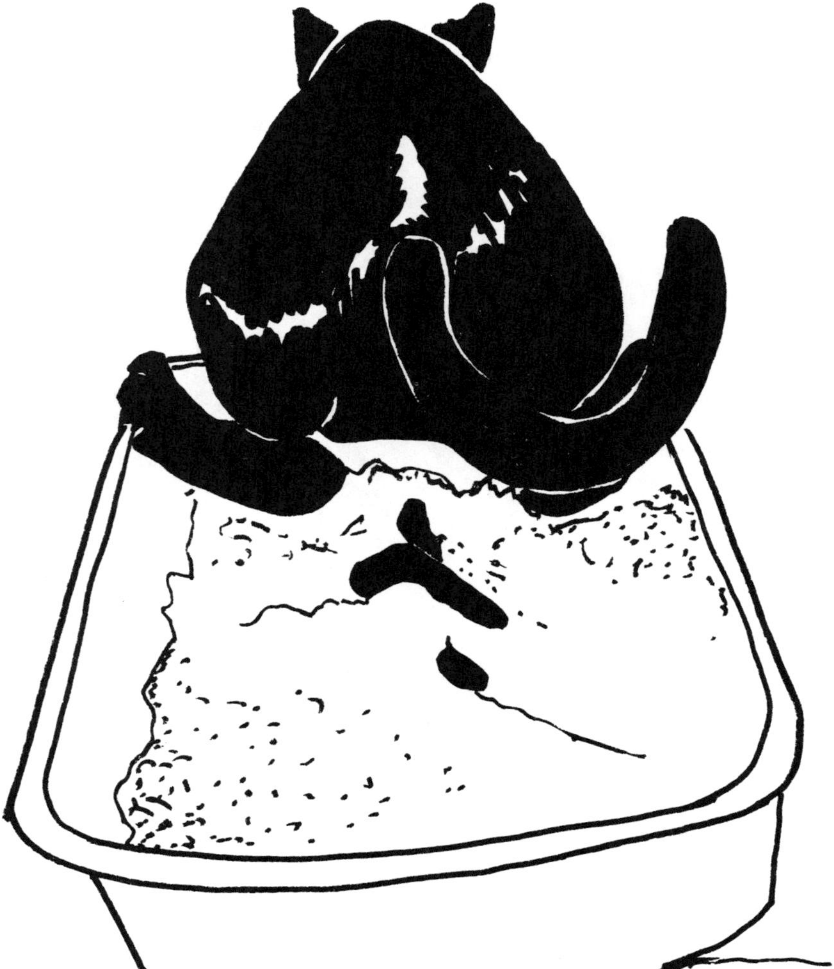

"Boo-Boo"

Boo-Boo's got a special flair.
He takes aim from in the air.

Once he tried it from the chair...

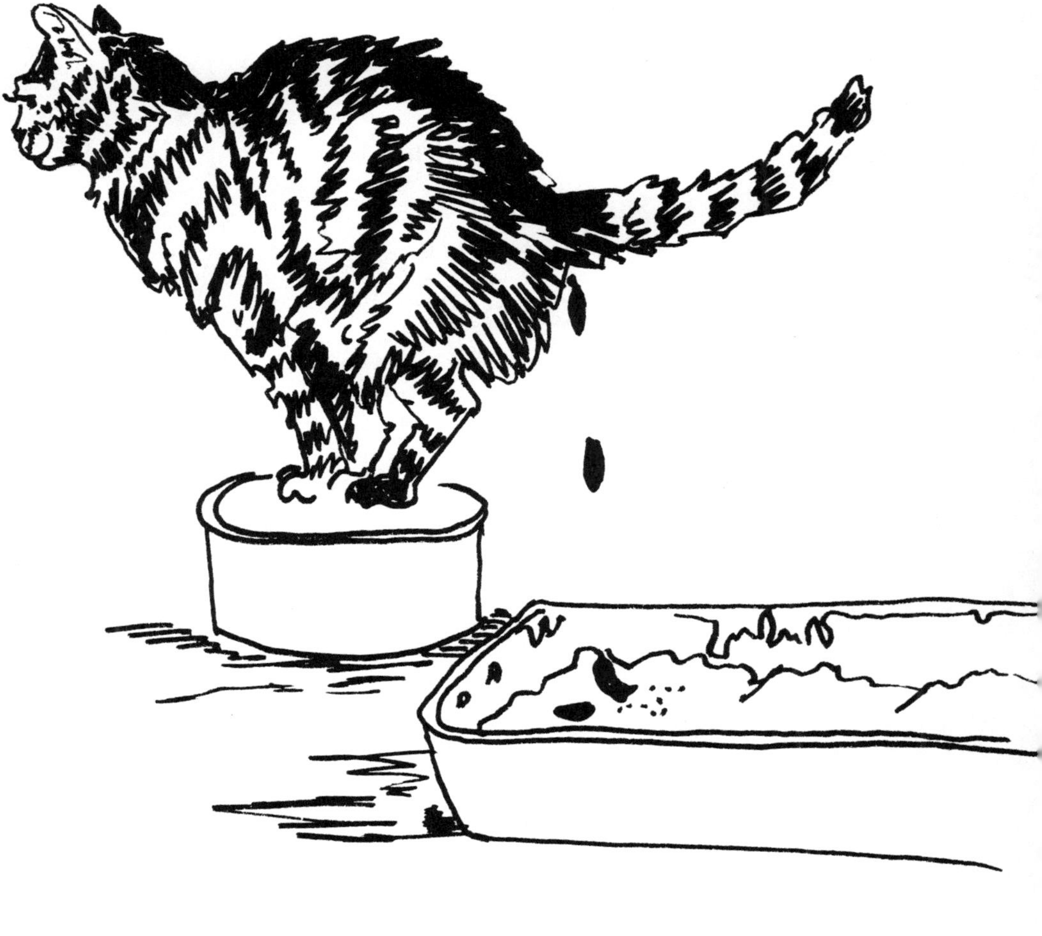

Oops!

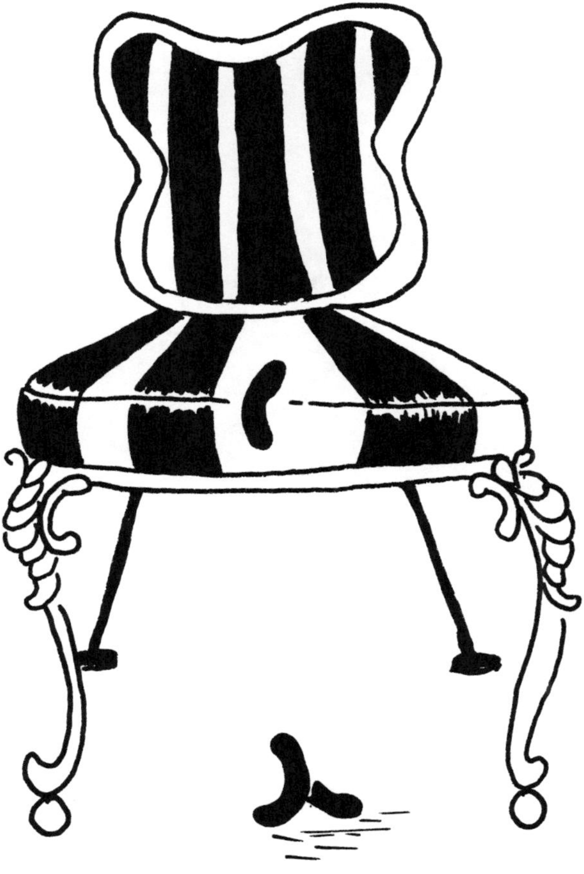

Now you know why we call him "Boo-Boo".

//"CoCoA"//

**Cocoa's virtue we extol
He can do it in the Bowl!**

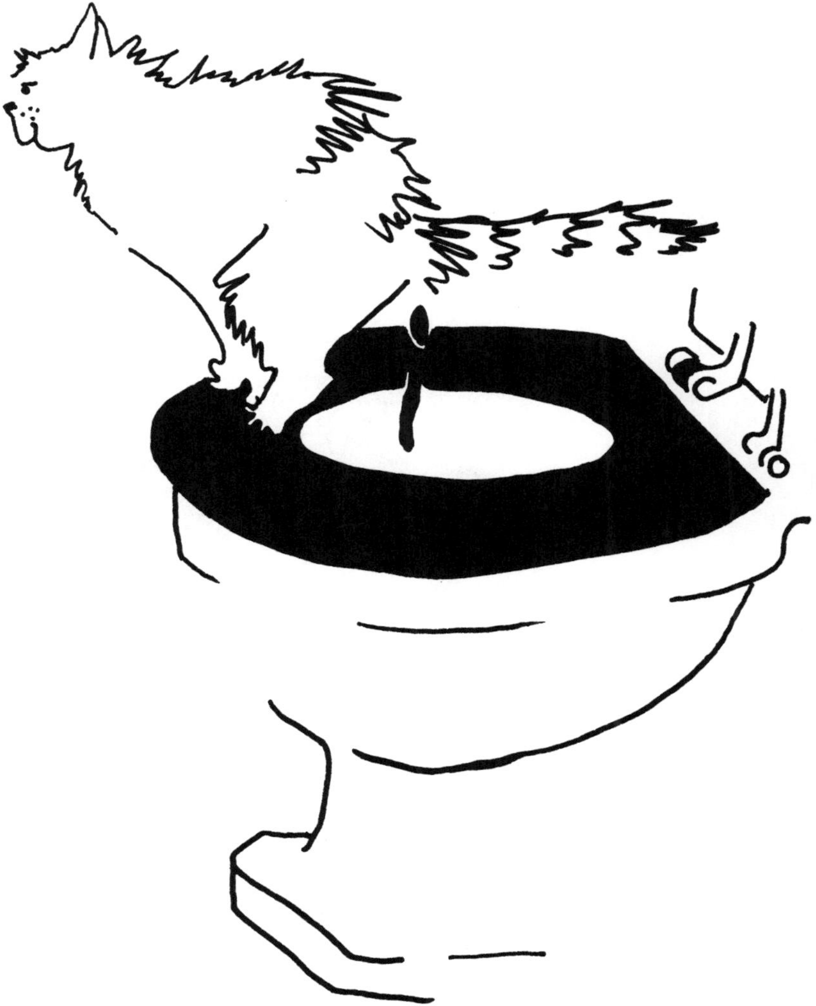

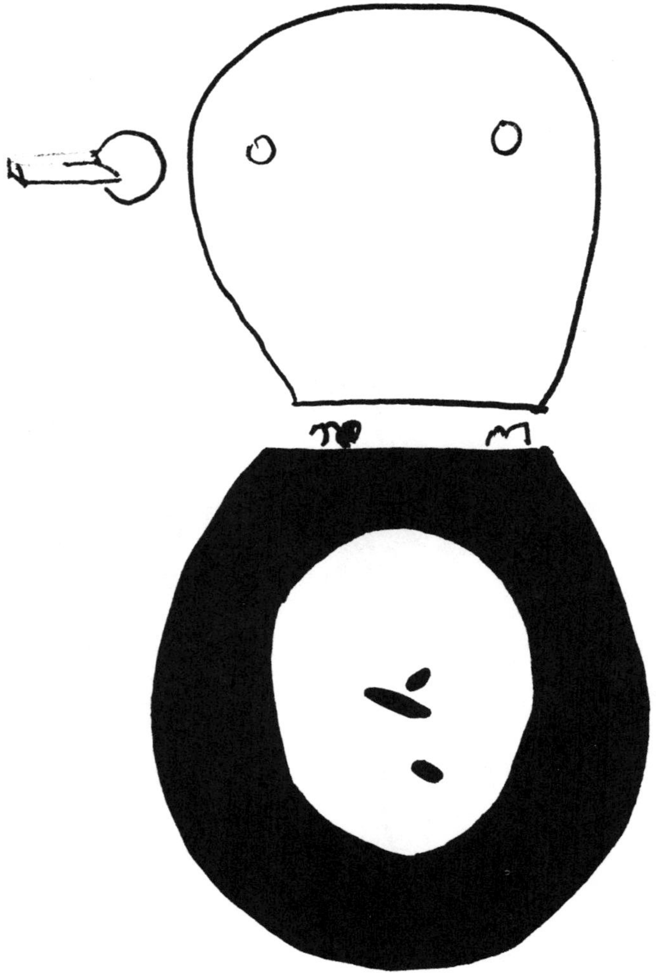

"Pouge"

Pouge (rhymes with rouge)
His nose is pink.
His coat is red.
And he sometimes likes to
Pee in bed...

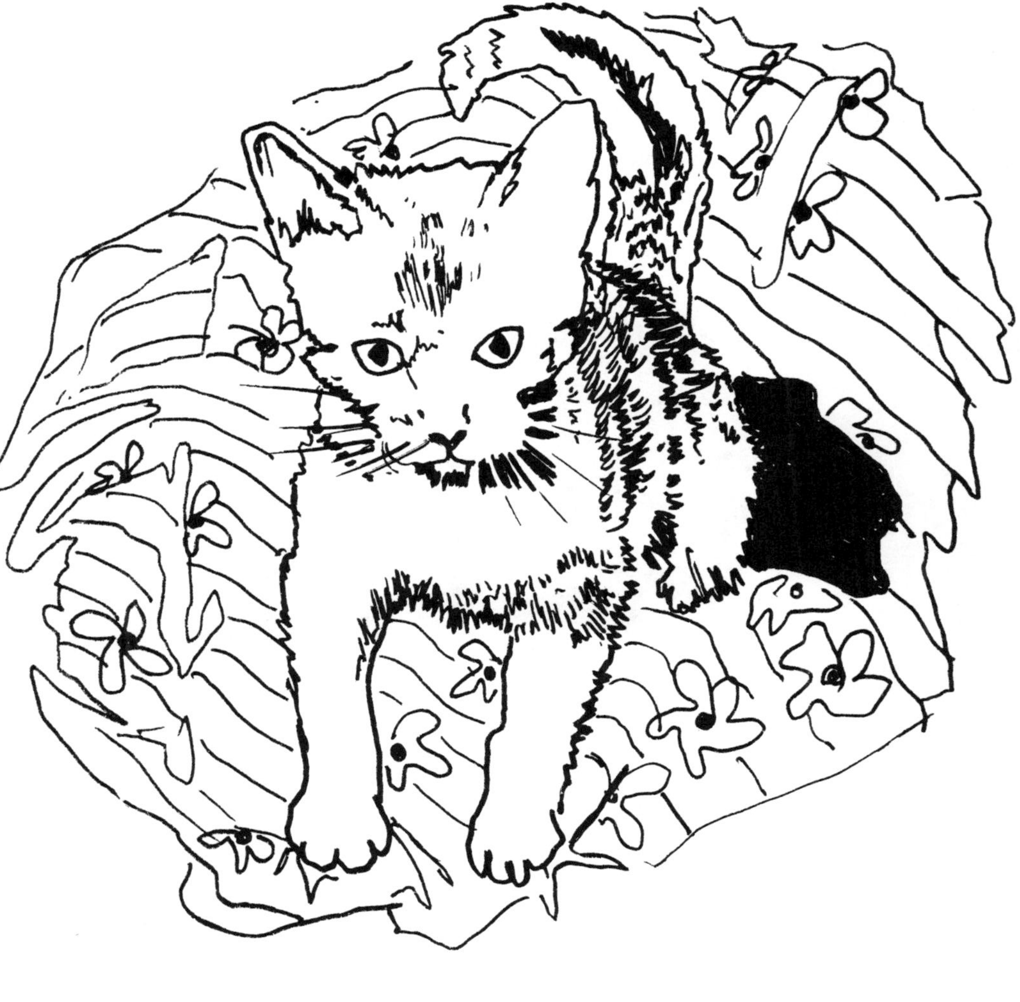

Just rolled over on a wet one...

Yuk!

"HAIRY"

**Hairy is a Yorkie
Whose tastes are a bit quorkie.**

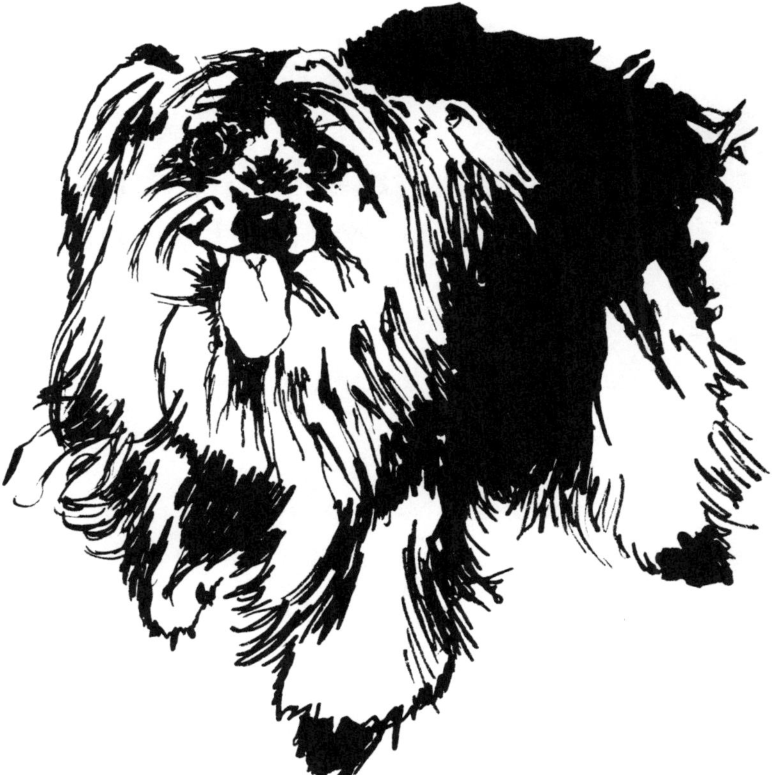

**His visits to the litterbox
Have made him more than porkie!**

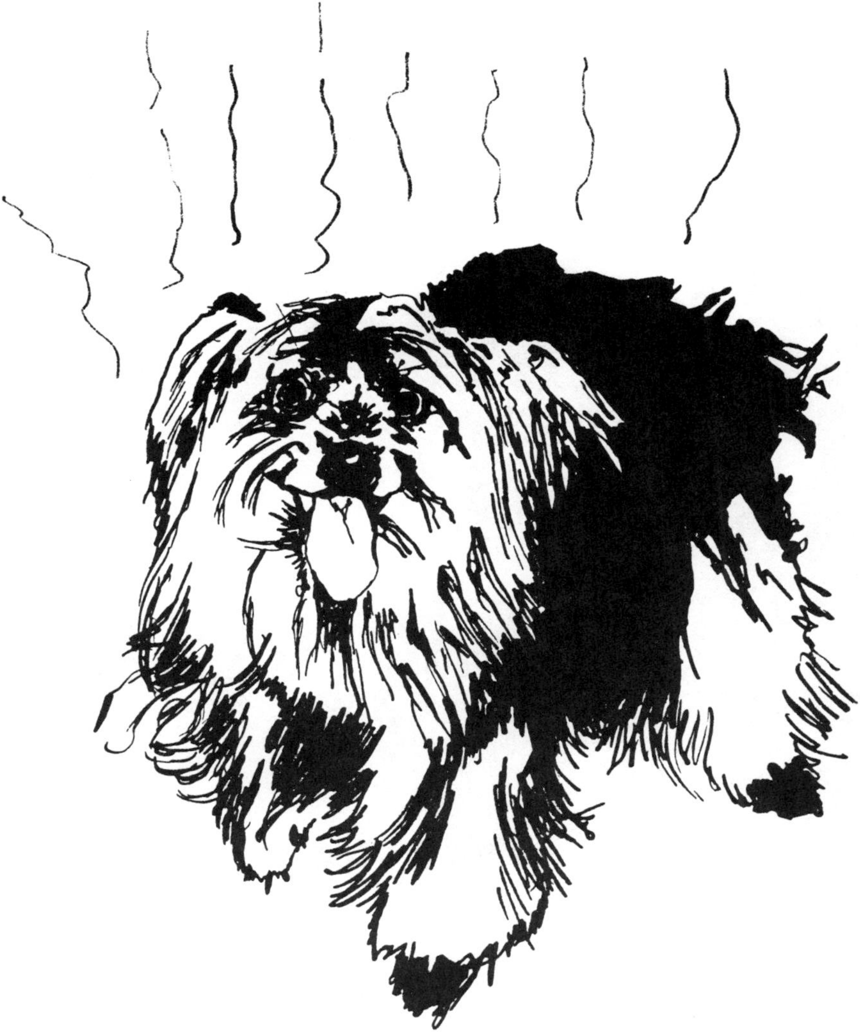

"Ma... I've gotta go!"

Three: *Litter-ally Speaking*

THE *LITTER* BOX!

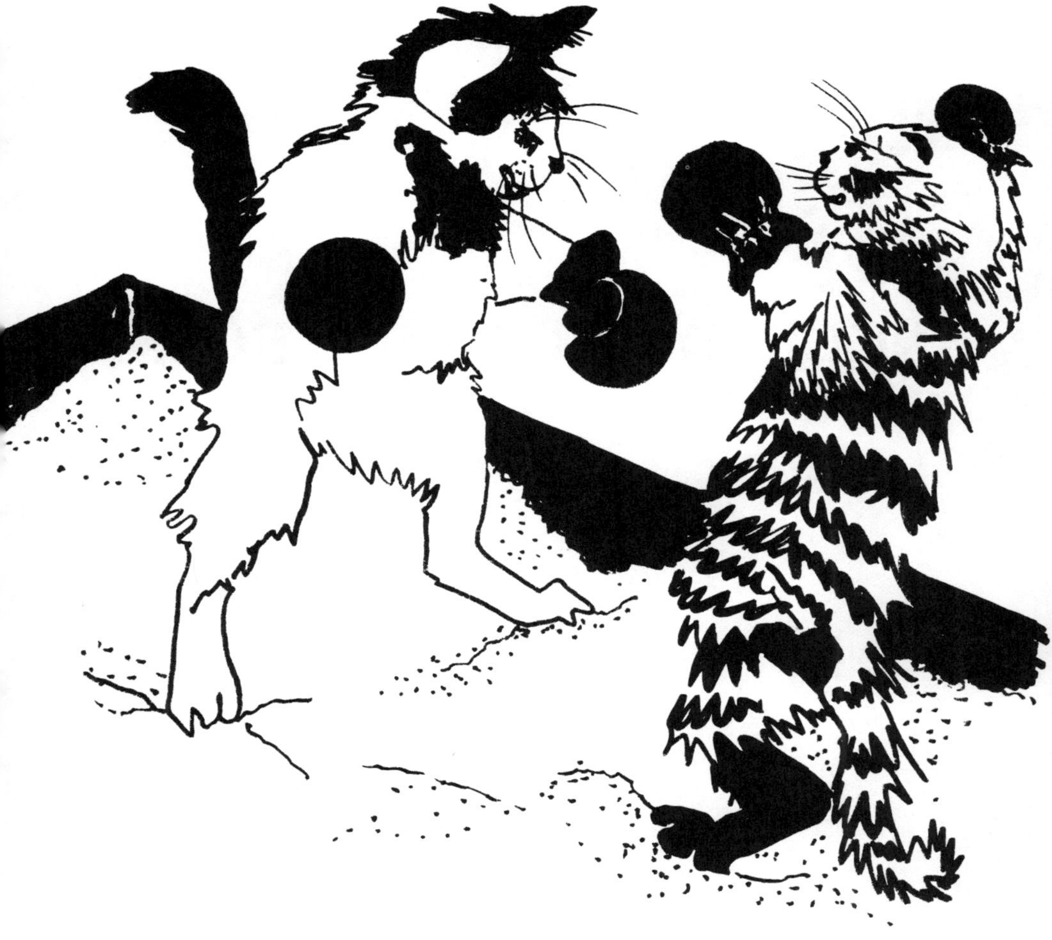

KNOCKED OUT OF THE *BOX!*

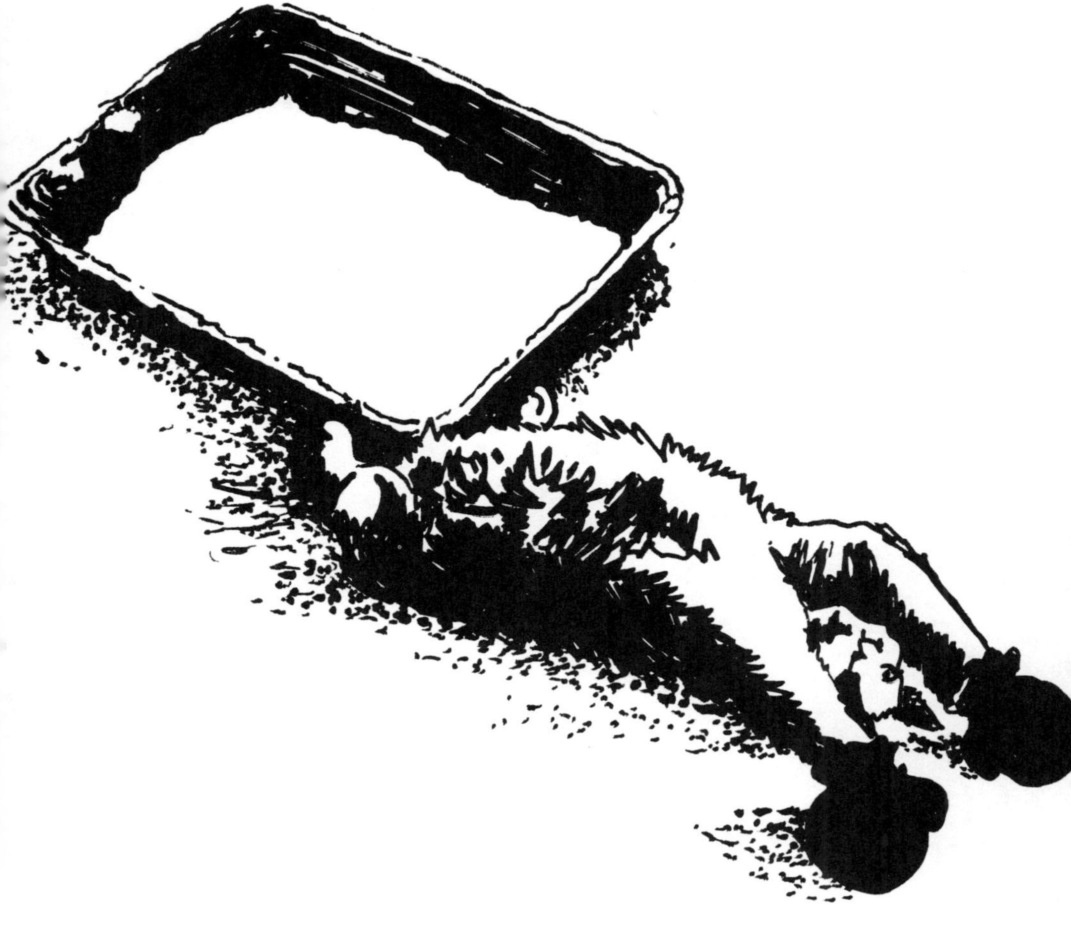

LITTER-MATES
(OR A *LITTER* LOVING)

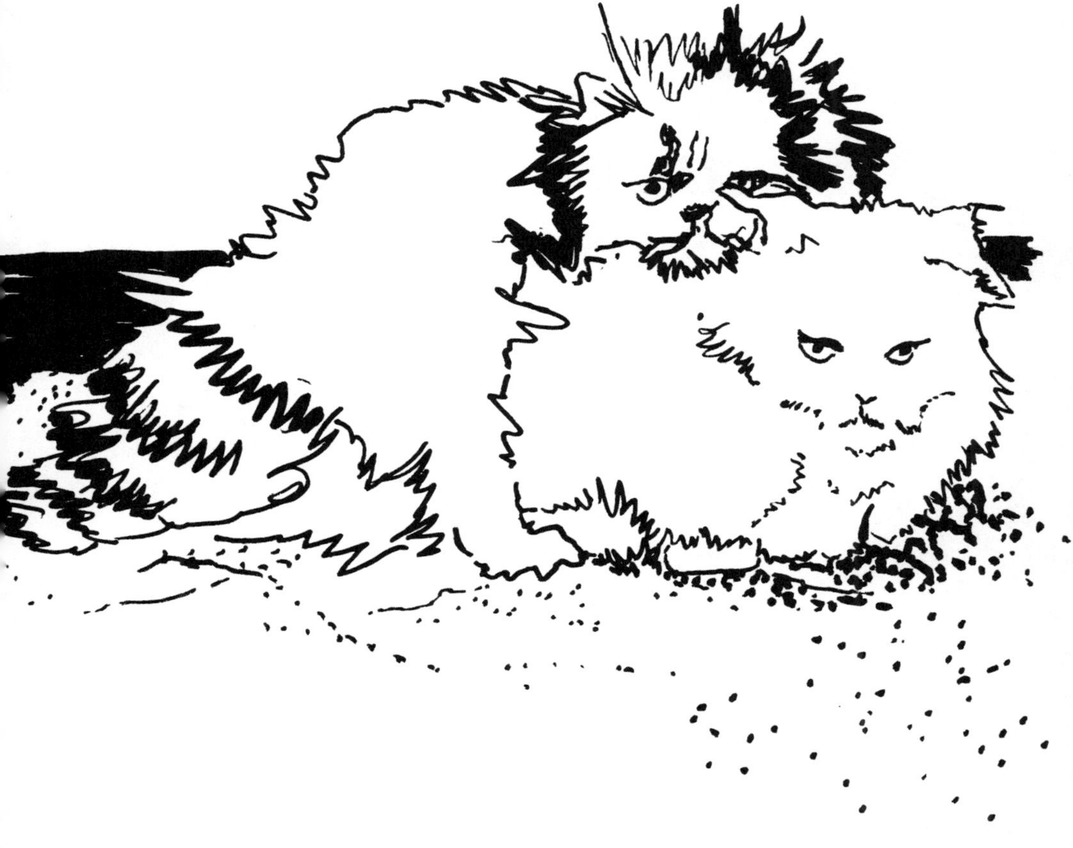

LITTA-GANTS

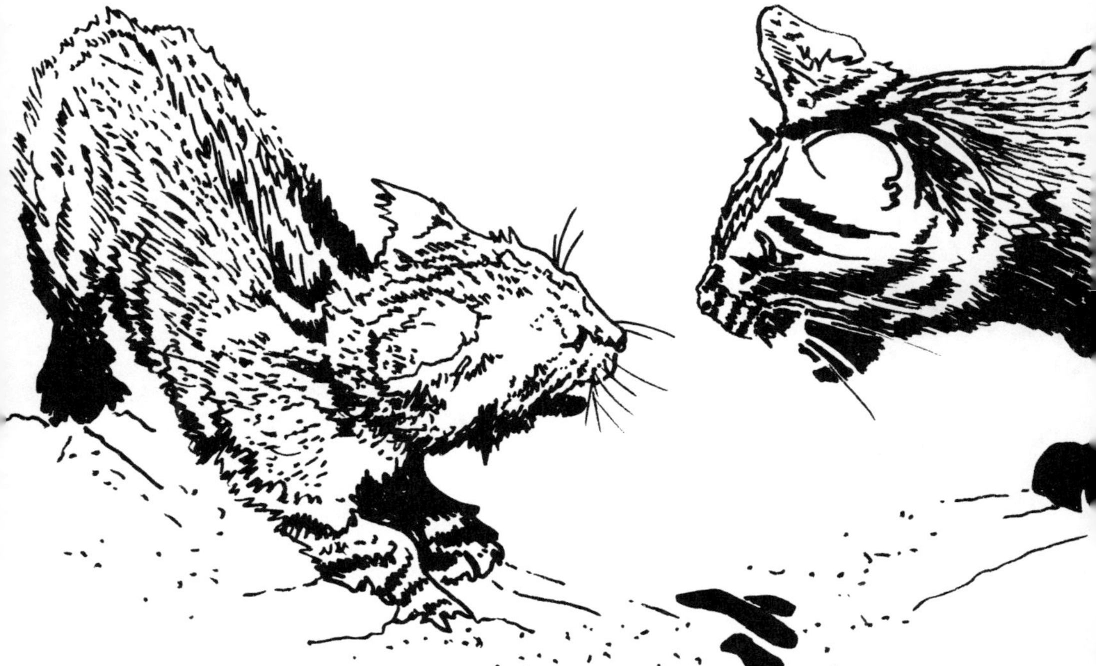

LITTER-ATURE

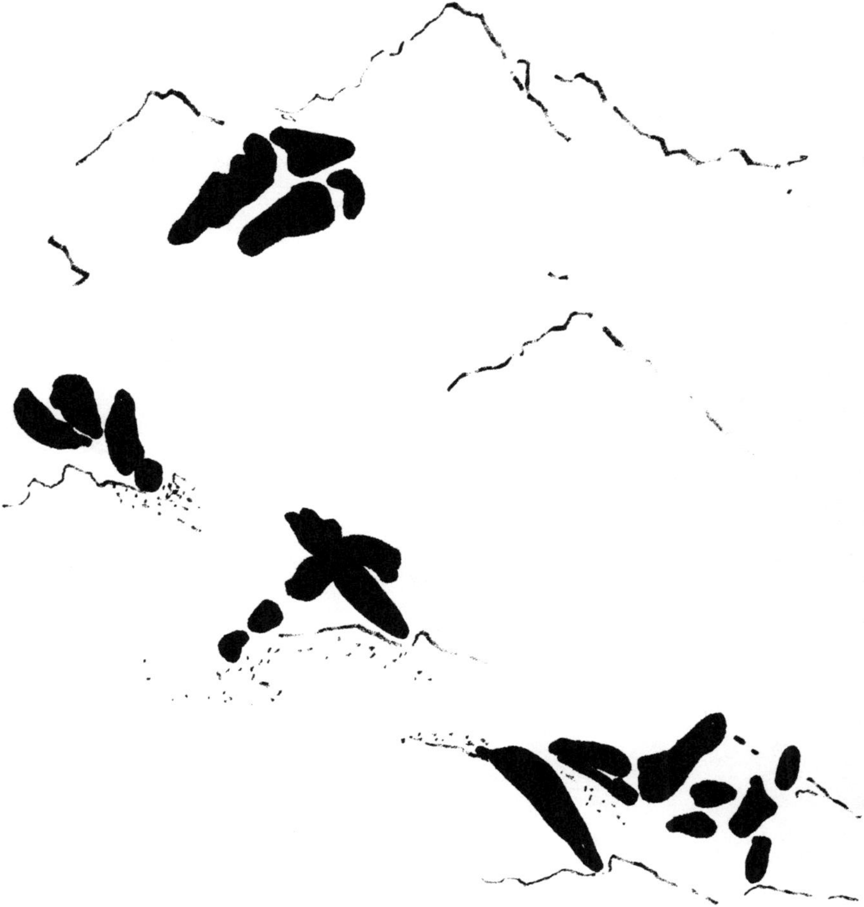

A *LITTER* BIT!

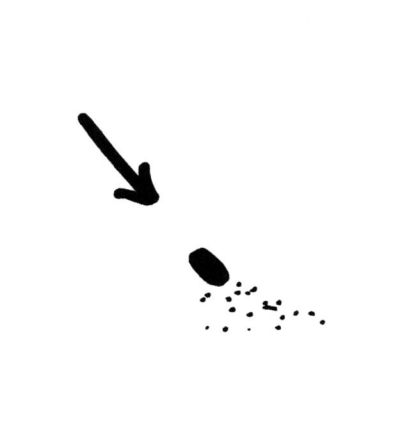

LITTER-AERIE

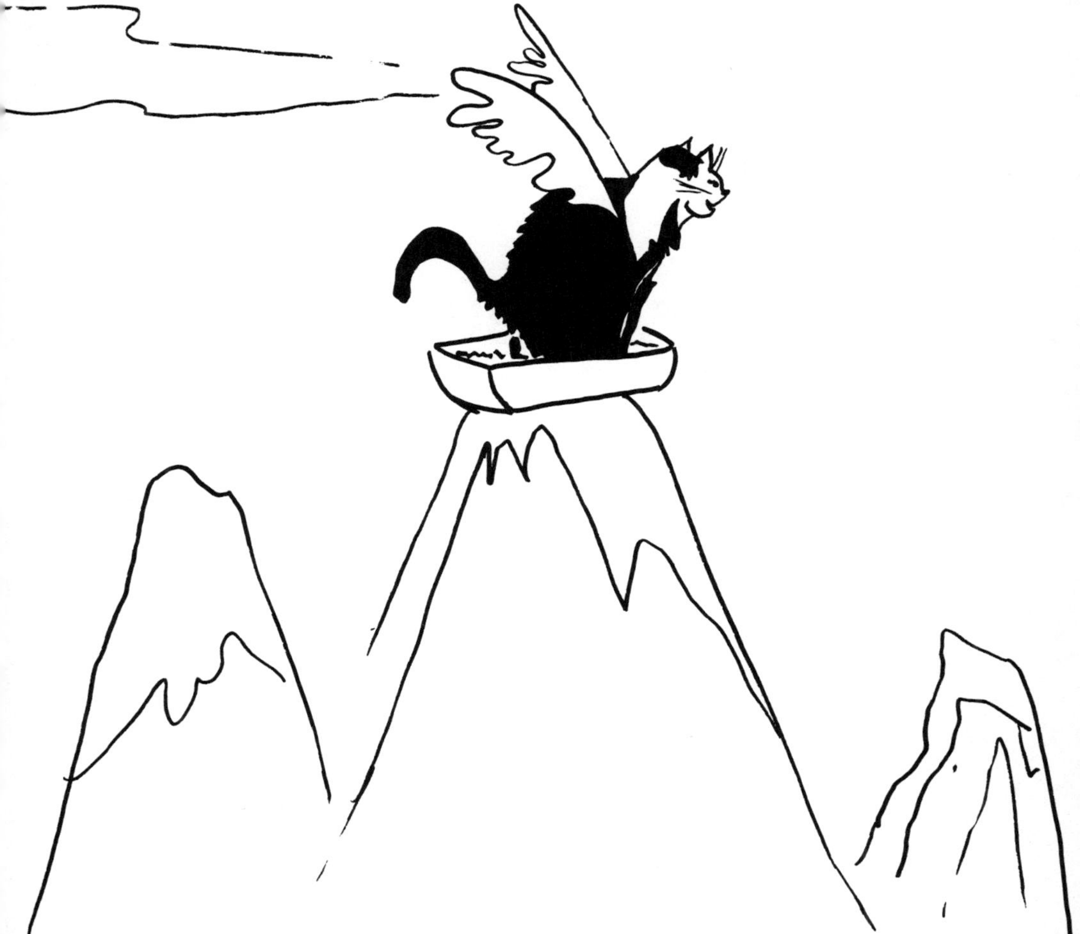

LITTER-BUGS!

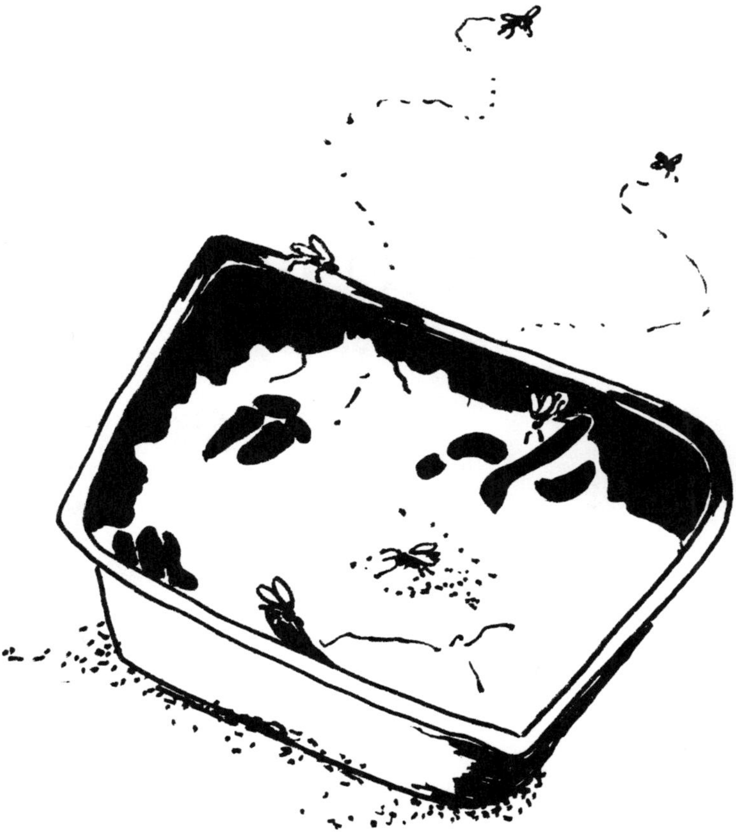

LITTER-BUGS
(CLOSE-UP)

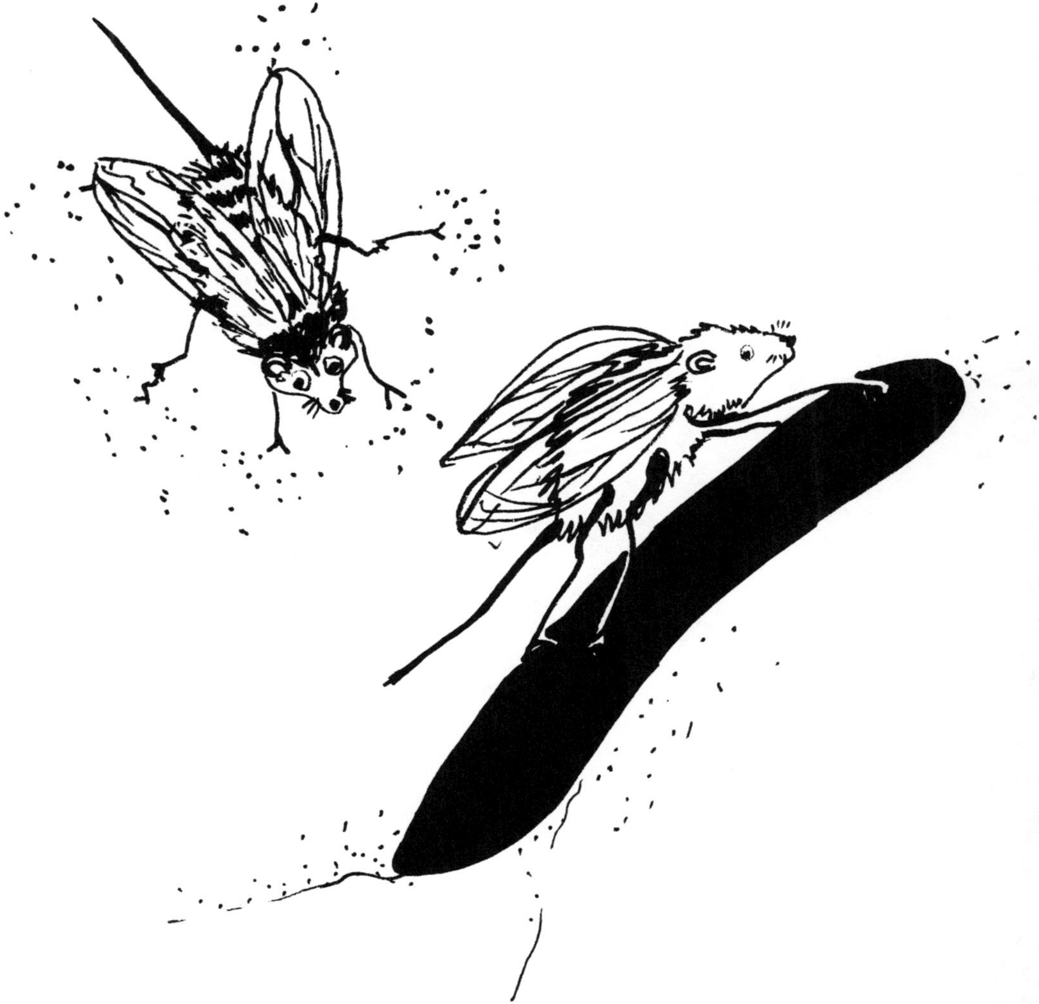

LITTER-ATE!

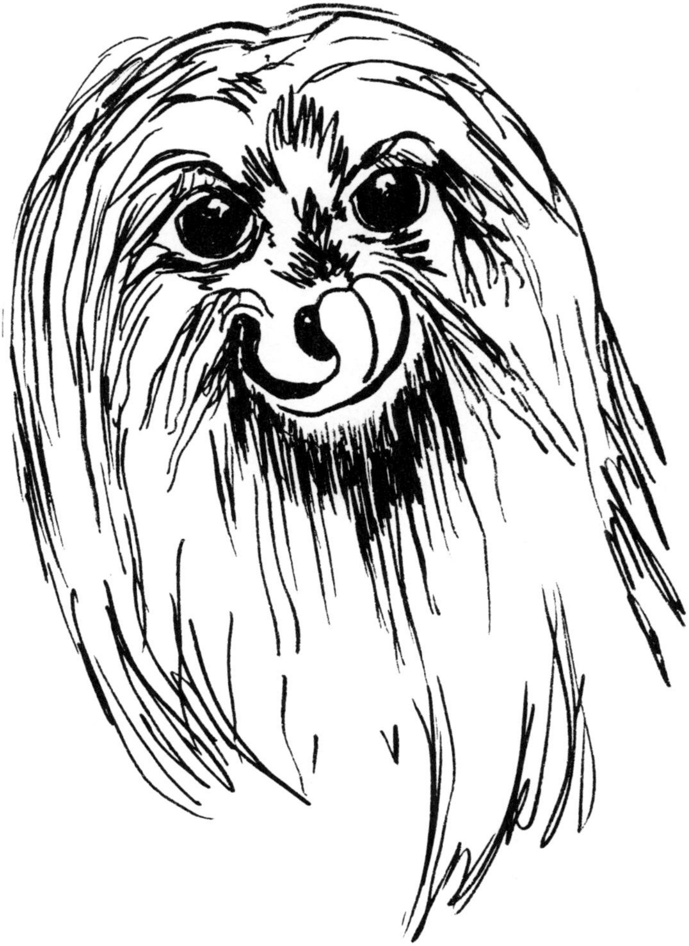

Four:
SCATT-ILLOGICAL REFERENCES

THE "COVER-UP"!

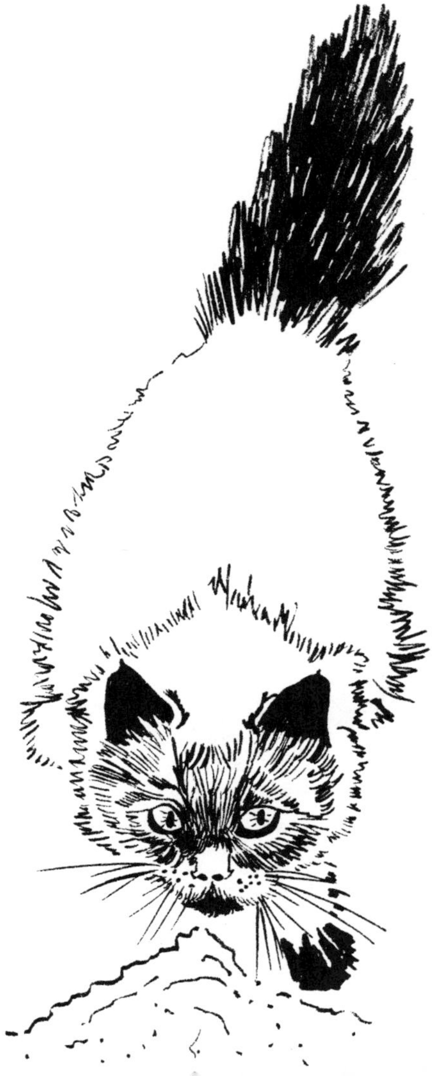

THE SMOKING GUN!

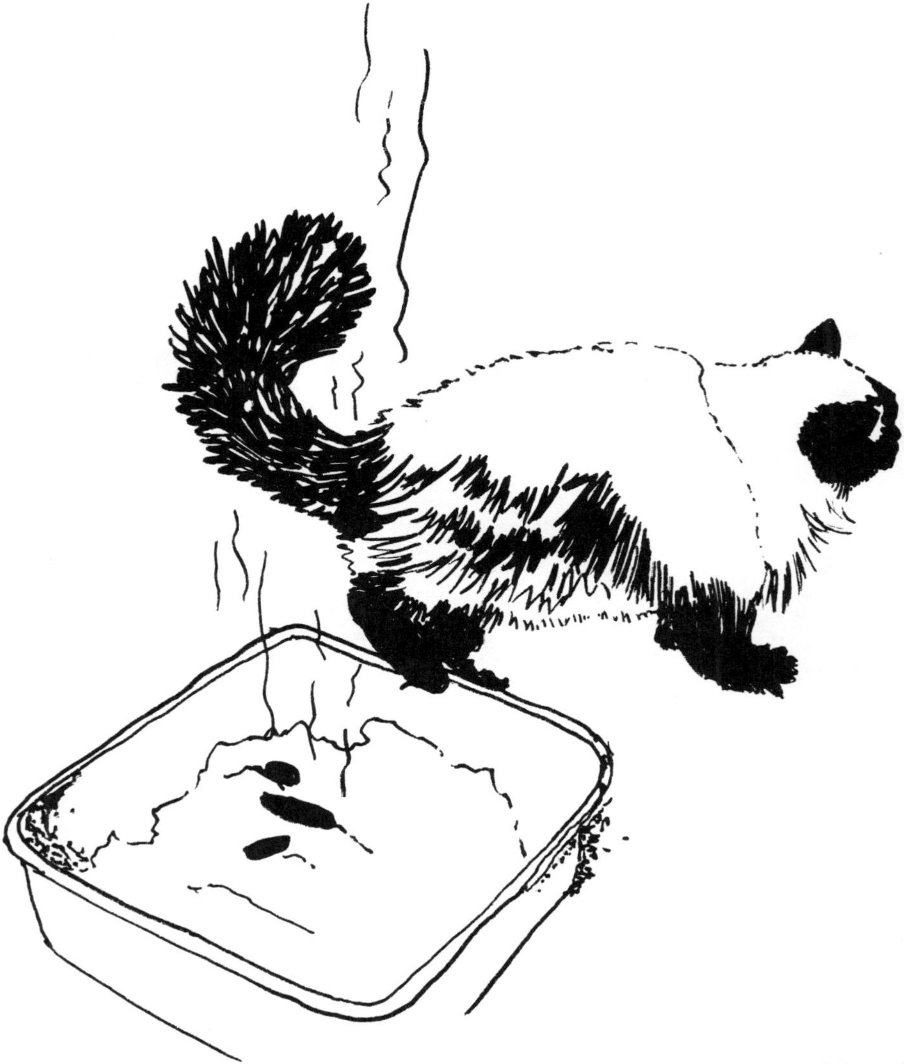

A *CRAP*-ITOL OFFENCE!

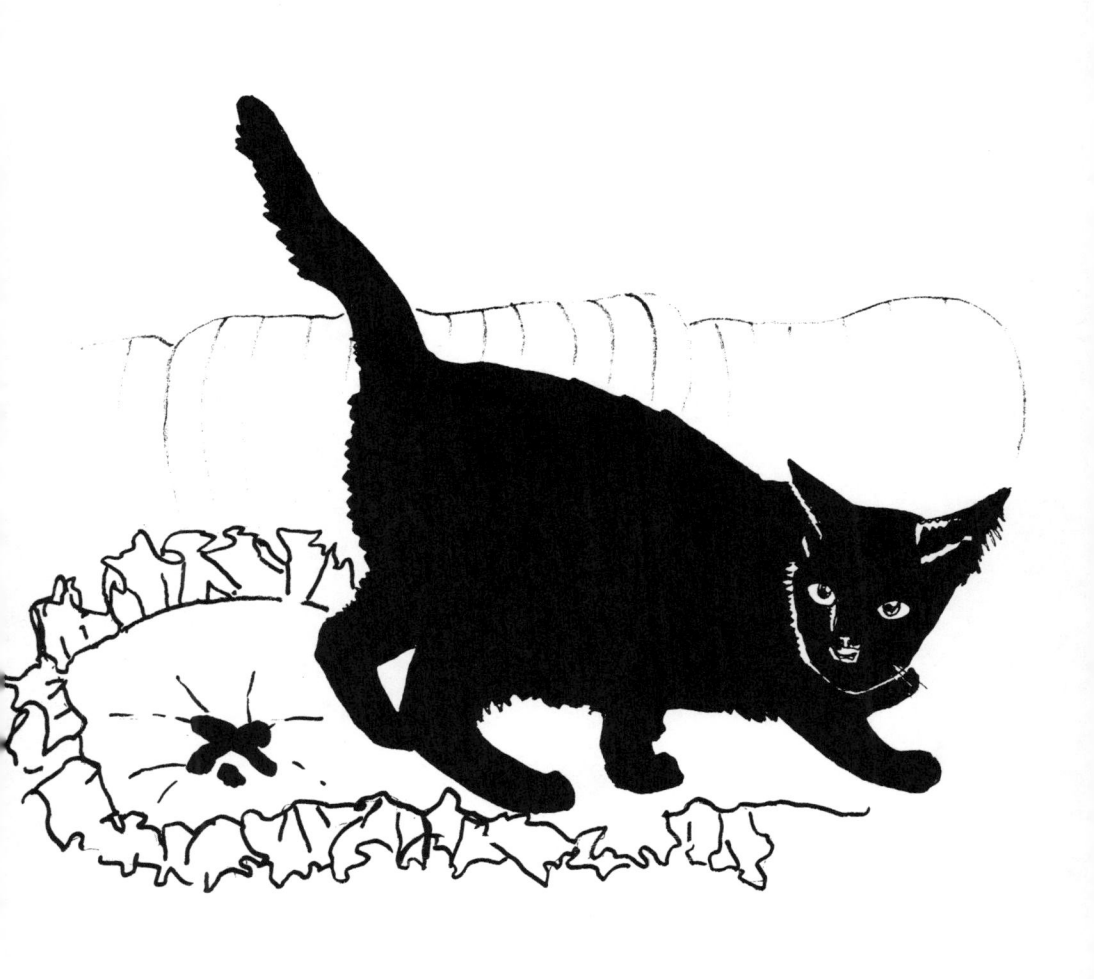

THE REAL "POOP" ON PERSIANS!

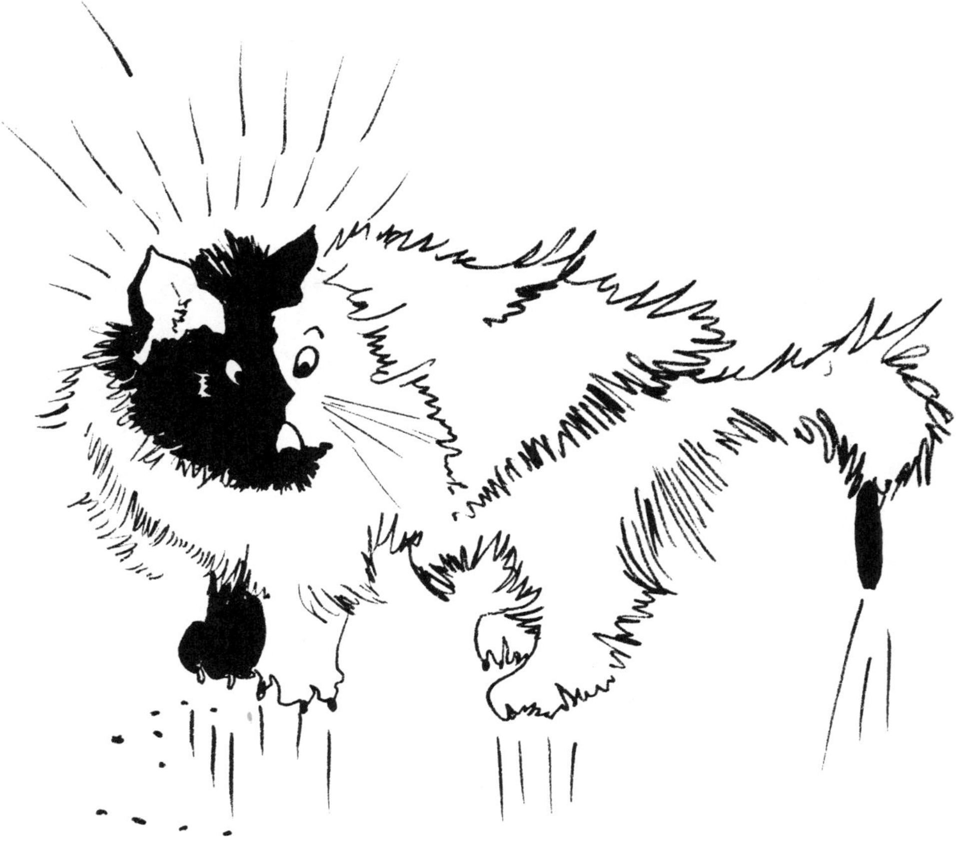

GETTING READY FOR THE BIG *BLOW-OUT!*

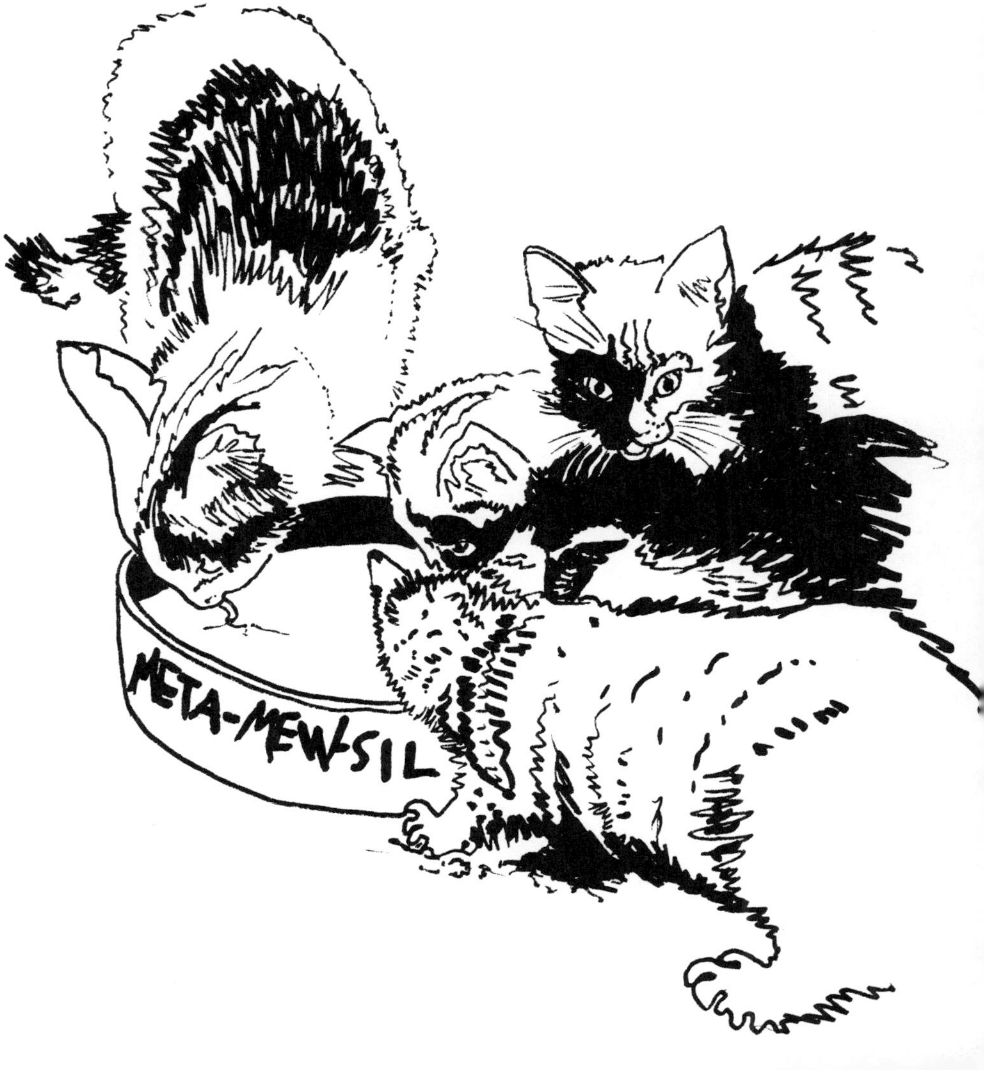

META-MEW-SIL

THE *CATTY*-CORNER

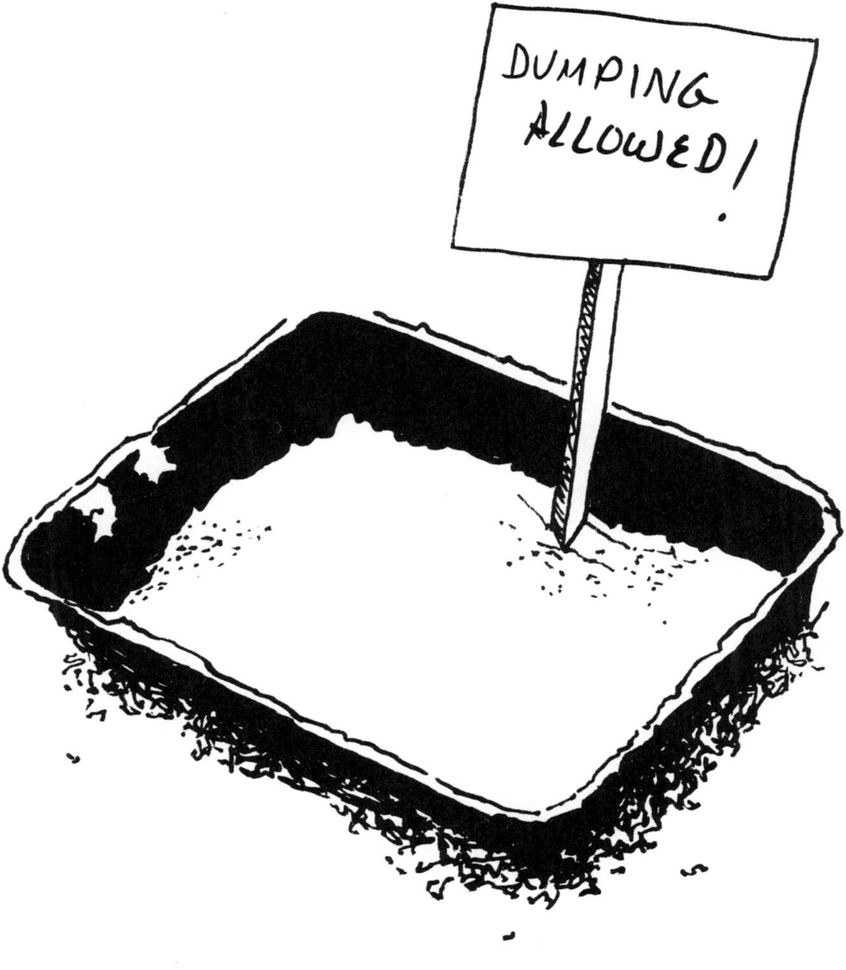
DUMPING
ALLOWED!

SMORGAS-BOX

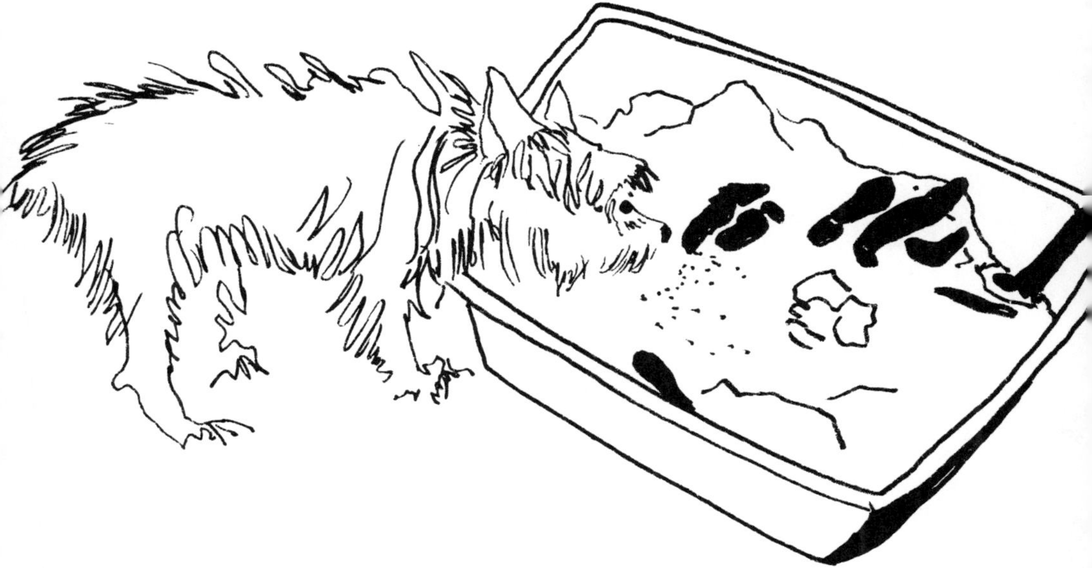

ONE SCOOP?

OR TWO?

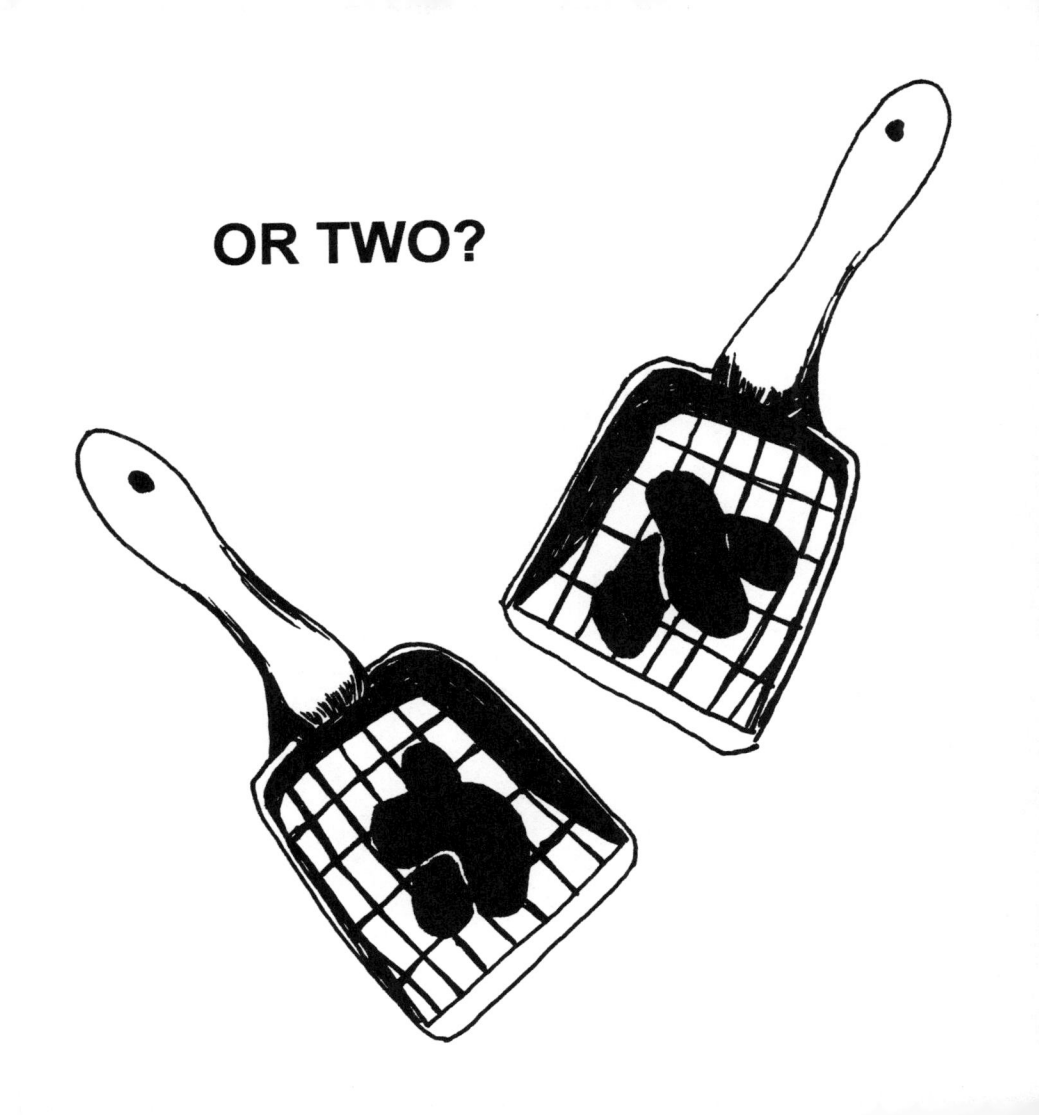

TIDY-BOWL

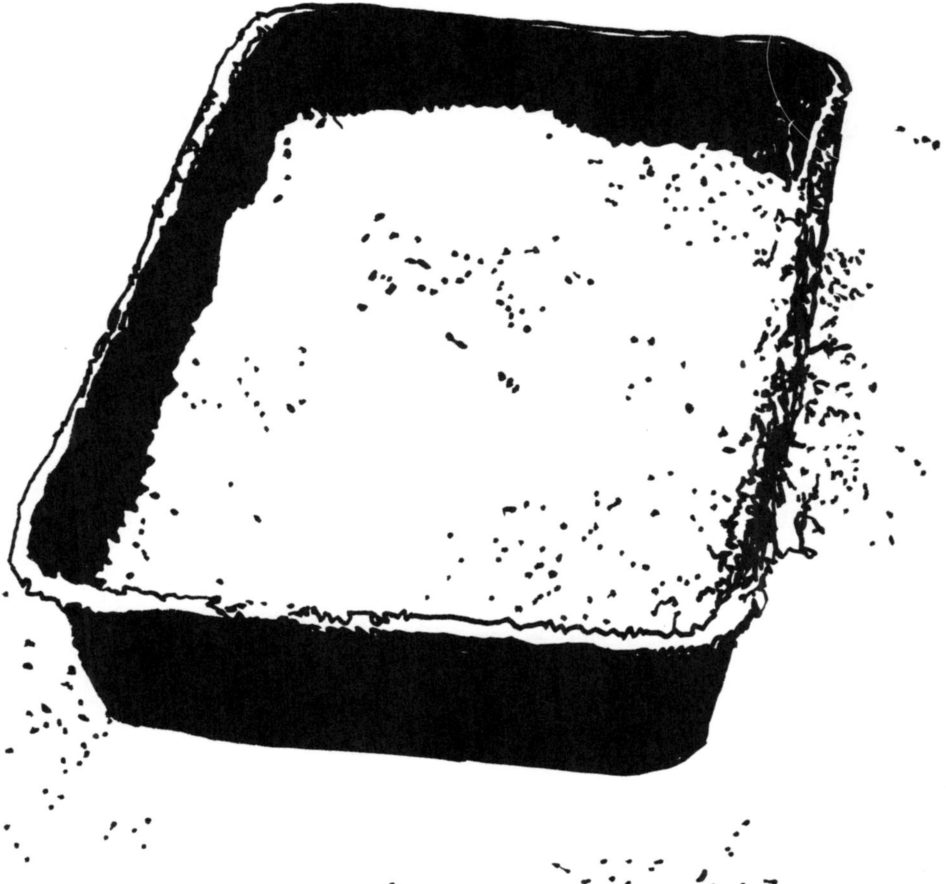

**THREE BOXES,
NO WAITING.**

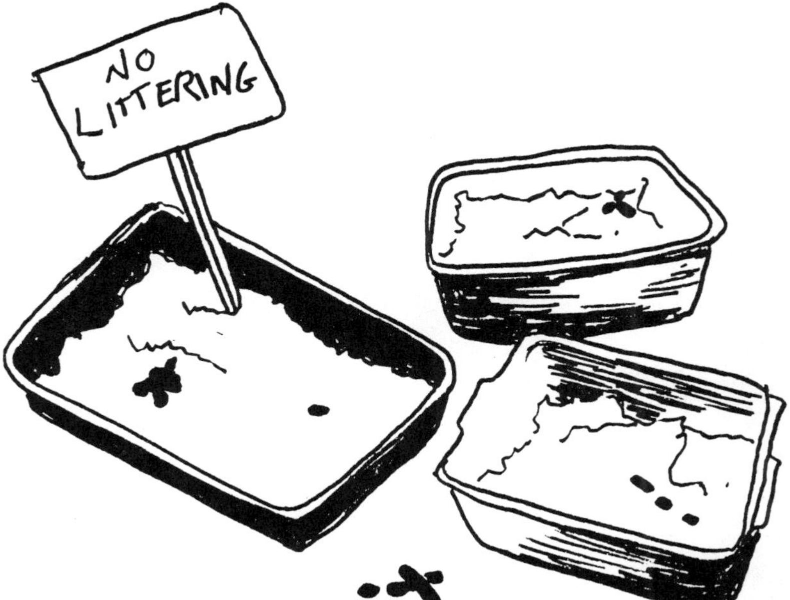
NO LITTERING

THE *SANDS OF TIME*...

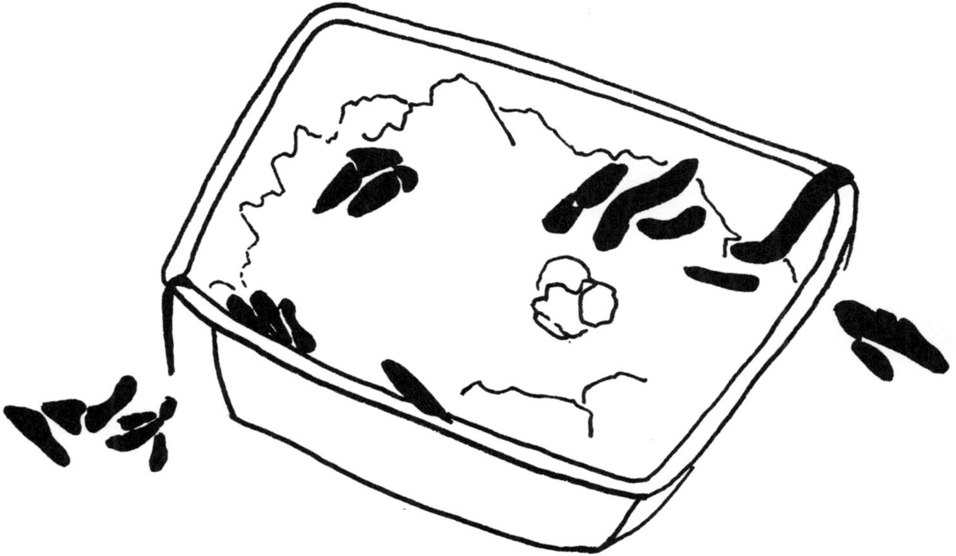

SAND "CASTINGS"

Sand Bar

Sand Dollar

A "Wheelie"

BOWLED OVER!

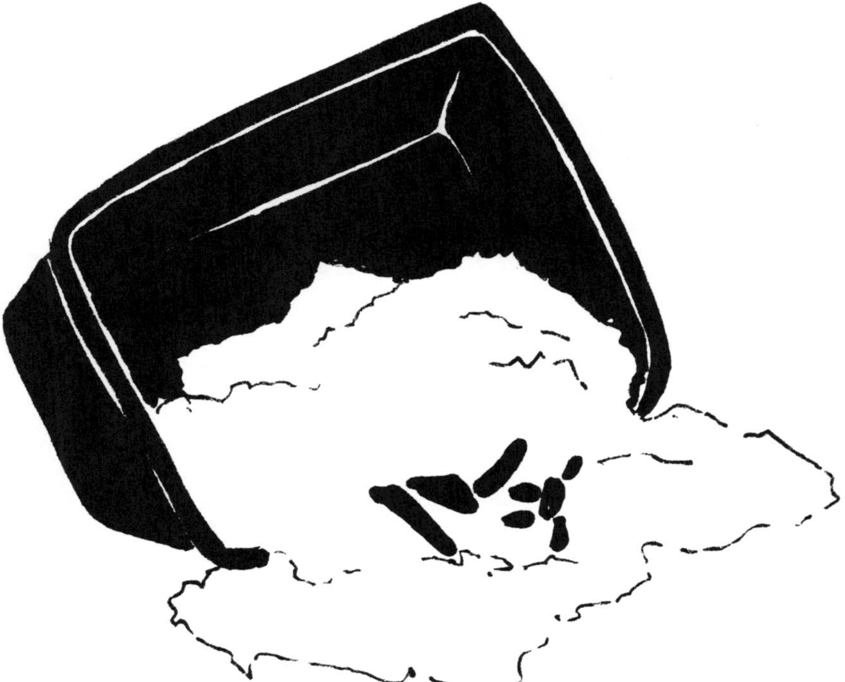

SANDY CLAWS!

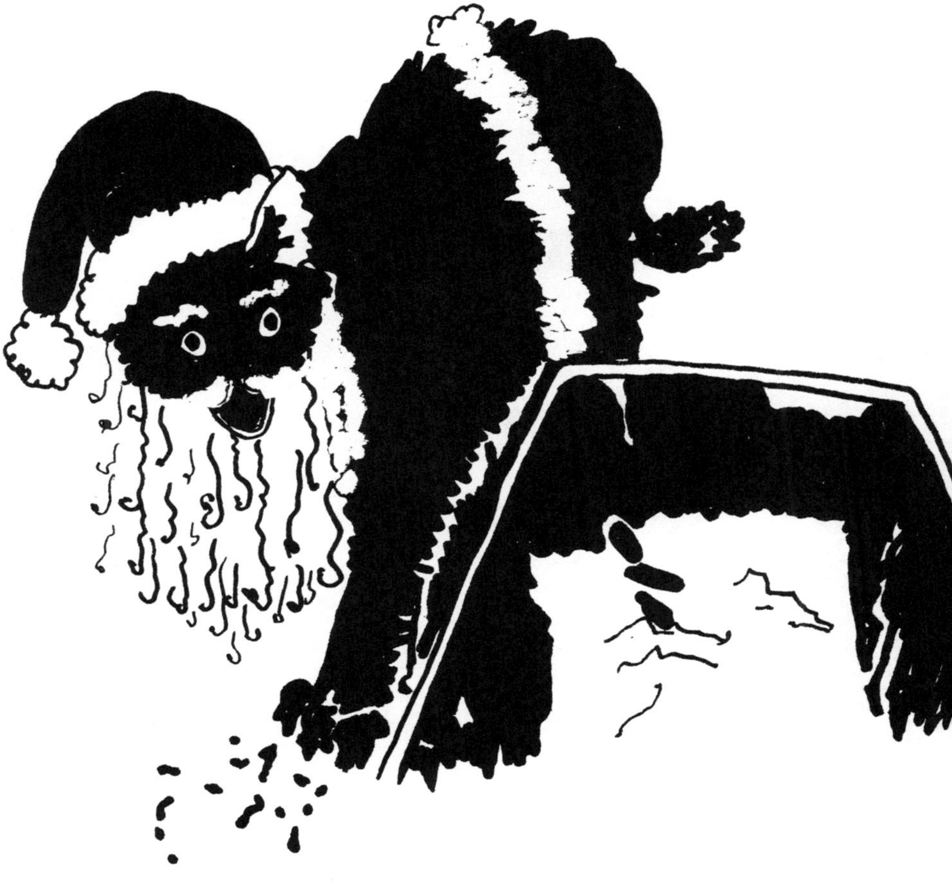

MRS. CLAWS

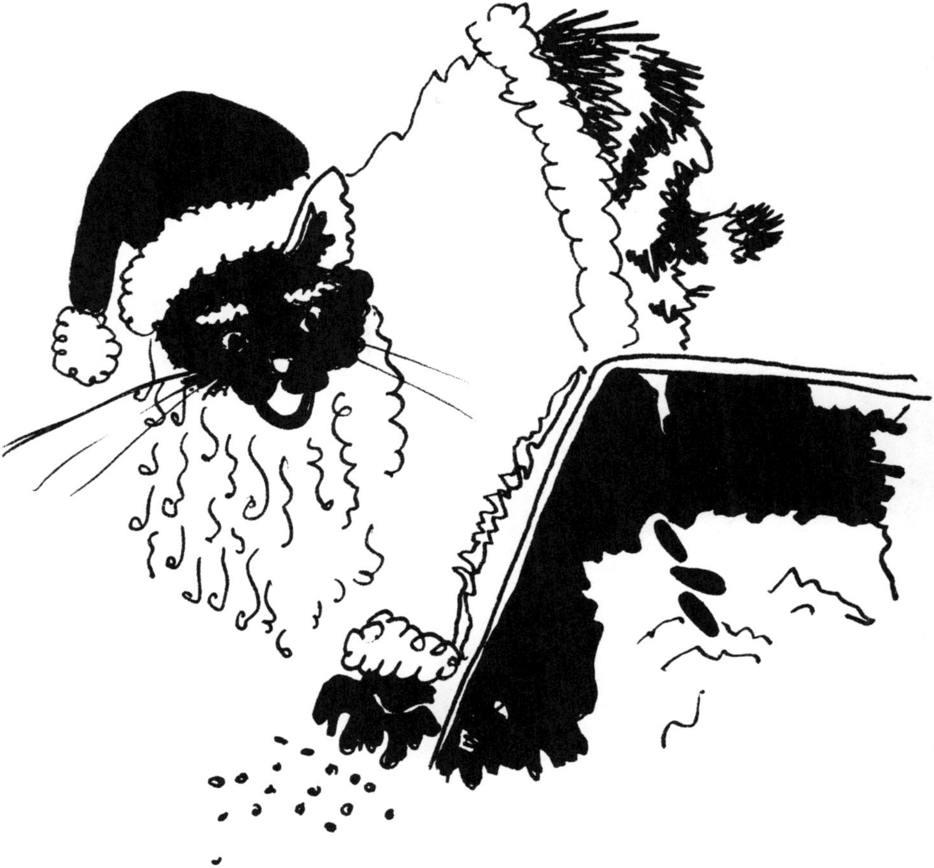

DESERT STORM!

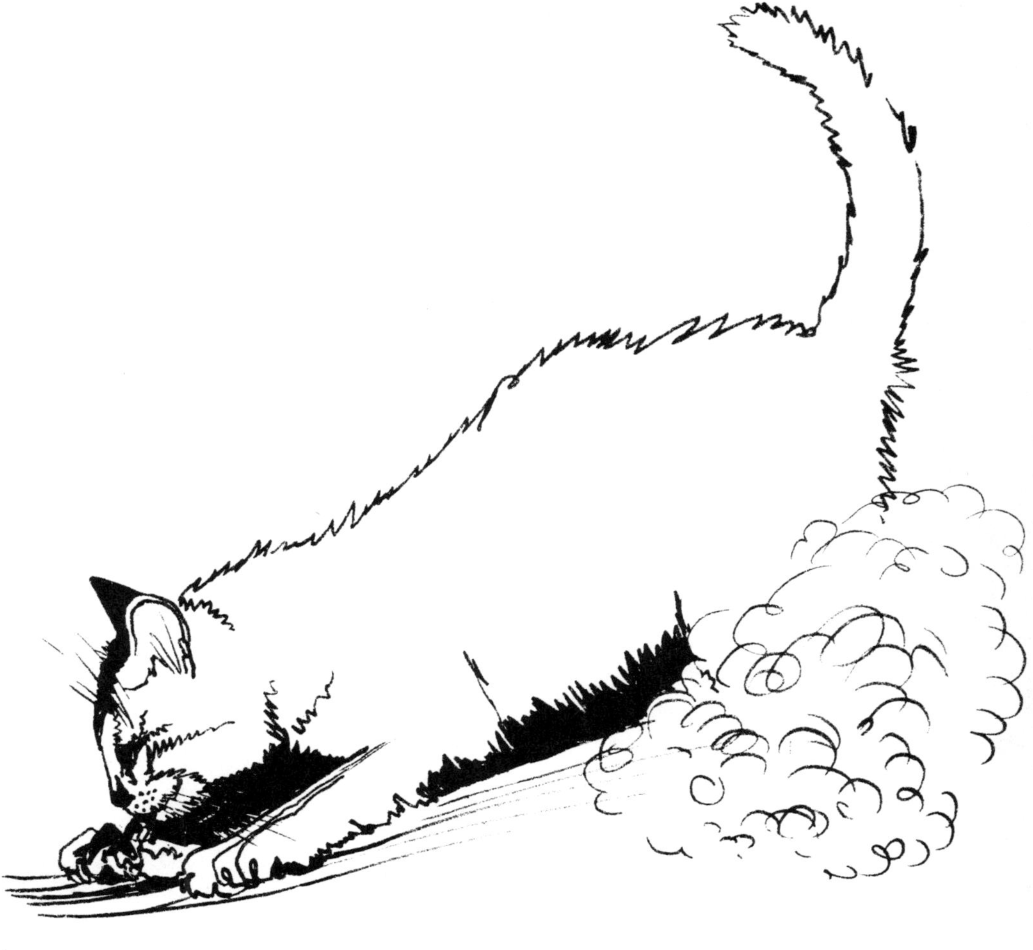

WINGING IT!

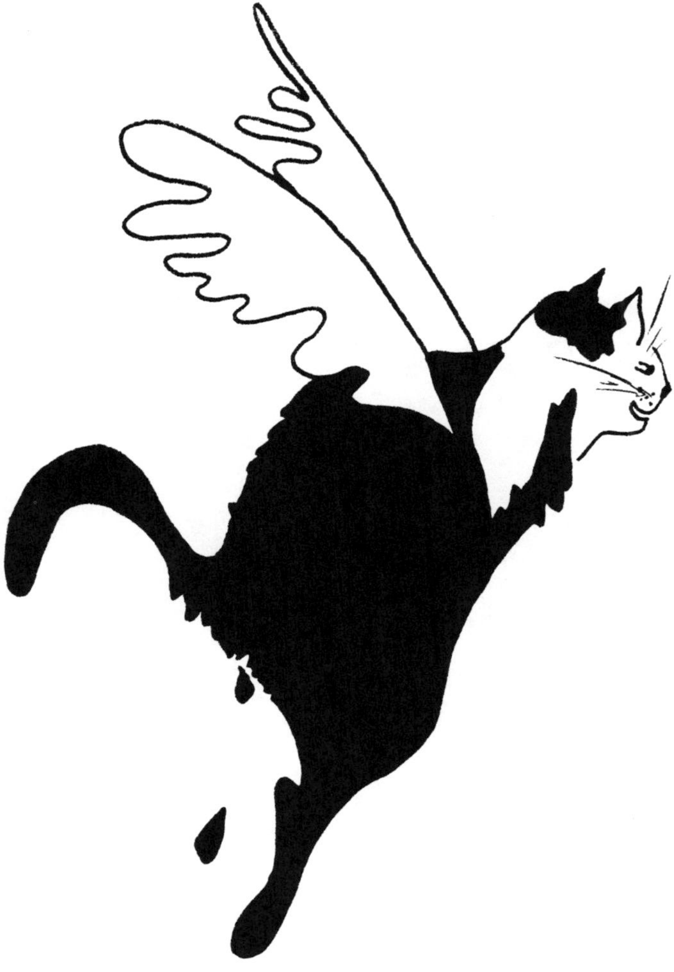

SOCIAL COMMENTARY

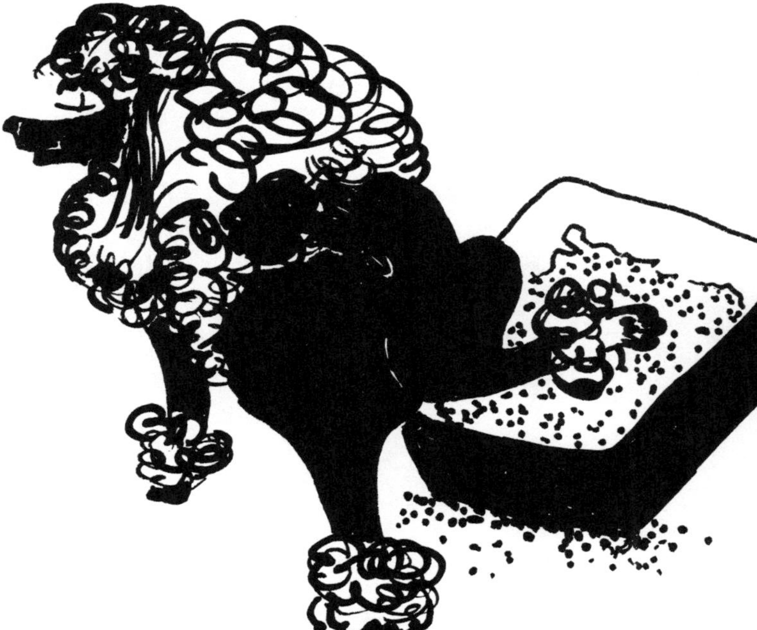

COMING SOON!

GIFTS THEY'LL NEVER FORGET
(even if they want to!)

FAT CAT SHAT™ STATIONARY and NOTE CARDS
(Comes in the "LitterBox" with Pen-scoop!)

FAT CAT SHAT™ POST CARDS

FAT CAT SHAT™ T-SHIRTS

FAT CAT SHAT™ CALENDAR
(For 12 months of *Crapschtick* Humor)

OTHER BOOKS & CASSETTES
by Julia Busch

POWER COLOR!
How to Attract Romance, Wealth,
Youth, Vitality and More!
with Hollye Davidson
(Kosmic Kurrents) $14.95

TREAT YOUR FACE LIKE A SALAD!
Skin Care Naturally, Wrinkle-and-Blemish-Free Recipes and
Hints for a Fabu-lishous Face! $14.95

FACELIFT NATURALLY
The At-Home or Anywhere, Painless, Natural Facelift for
Men and Women That Really Works!
Audio kit: book, charts $59.98   Book only $14.95

POSITIVELY YOUNG!
The How to Live, Love, Laugh, Let-Go and Erase *INNER WRINKLES* at Any Age Game Book for Men and Women
2 cassettes/2 hours $24.95   Book $9.95

YOUTH AND SKIN SECRETS REVEALED!
What Your Face Can Tell on You and How You Can Change What it is Saying!
One hour audio program $19.95

Free Brochure and Information
1 800 SO YOUNG
or write to:
Anti-Aging Press
P.O. Box 141489
Coral Gables, FL 33114 USA